W9-DGC-129

AMERICA'S DISAPPEARED

AMERICA'S DISAPPEARED
Detainees, Secret Imprisonment, and the "War on Terror"

Edited by
Rachel Meeropol

with Reed Brody, Barbara Olshansky,
Michael Ratner, and Steven Macpherson Watt

An Open Media Book
SEVEN STORIES PRESS
New York • London • Toronto • Melbourne

A Seven Stories Press First Edition

Open Media Series Editor: Greg Ruggiero

Seven Stories Press
140 Watts Street
New York, NY 10013
www.sevenstories.com

In Canada:
Publishers Group Canada, 250A Carlton Street, Toronto, ON M5A-2L1

In the UK:
Turnaround Publisher Services Ltd., Unit 3, Olympia Trading Estate, Coburg Road, Wood Green, London N22 6TZ

In Australia:
Palgrave Macmillan, 627 Chapel Street, South Yarra VIC 3141

Library of Congress Cataloging-in-Publication Data

America's disappeared : detainees, secret imprisonment, and the "War on Terror" / edited by Rachel Meeropol, with Reed Brody ... [et al.].-- 1st ed.
    p. cm. -- (An open media book)
  Includes bibliographical references and index.
  ISBN 1-58322-645-1 (pbk. : alk. paper)
  1. Political prisoners--United States. 2. Muslims--Legal status, laws, etc.--United States. 3. Muslims--Civil rights--United States. 4. Arab Americans--Legal status, laws, etc. 5. Arab Americans--Civil rights. 6. War on Terrorism, 2001- --Social aspects. 7. War on Terrorism, 2001---Political aspects. 8. War on terrorism, 2001- --United States. I. Meeropol, Rachel. II. Brody, Reed, 1953- III. Series.
  HV9471.A484 2004
  973.931--dc22   2004028028

College professors may order examination copies of Seven Stories Press titles for a free six-month trial period. To order, visit www.sevenstories.com/textbook, or fax on school letterhead to (212) 226-1411.

Book design by Jon Gilbert
Cover design by Greg Ruggiero
Cover image by Micha Bar Am/Magnum Photos

Printed in Canada.

9 8 7 6 5 4 3 2 1

Contents

Dedicated to the memory of Farouk Abdel-Muhti and to the millions of others who remain locked down behind prison walls, on strike in immigration centers and shackled in wire cages. If you keep fighting, so will we.

Acknowledgments

FIRST AND FOREMOST, we wish to thank all our colleagues at the Center for Constitutional Rights for the incredible work that they have done on the cases described in this book, and their tireless efforts to safeguard the Constitution in the wake of the September 11 attacks. Special thanks to Marc Krupanski, for spending hours editing and adding to this manuscript, to Jen Nessel and Bob Osborne for their guidance through its production, Greg Ruggiero and the staff at Seven Stories Press for initiating this project and for their skillful and meticulous final edits, and to Jeff Fogel and Ron Daniels for their steadfast leadership in such a pivotal period.

Thanks also to the individual activists, attorneys, university professors, journalists, law firms, and other international and non-profit organizations, with whom we have worked over the past three years: Amnesty International, Human Rights Watch, Columbia University Human Rights Clinic, Desis Rising Up and Moving, Coney Island Avenue Project, Families for Freedom, ACLU, Immigrant Defense Project, New Immigrant Community Empowerment, American Friends Support Center, Islamic Council of North America, American-Arab Anti-discrimination Center, Asian American Legal Defense and Education Fund, Northern Manhattan Coalition for Immigrant Rights, Coalition for the Human Rights of Immigrants, Immigrant Justice Solidarity Project, Human Rights First, Immigration Equality, CAAAV: Organizing Asian Communities, Nodutdol—for Korean

Community Development, Quilombo NYC, Committee for the Release of Farouk Abdel-Muhti, New Jersey Civil Rights Defense Committee, Stop the Disappearances Campaign, and many others. It has been a privilege to work with you all and without your support and collaboration, our goal of preserving our civil and human rights in the post–September 11 era would be a whole lot more difficult.

We should also like to extend thanks to our clients, Shafiq Rasul, Asif Iqbal, Rhuel Ahmed, and the families of other detainees who remain in limbo at Guantánamo Bay, to Maher Arar and his wife and children, and to Ibrahim Turkmen, Shakir Baloch, Asif-Ur-Rehman Safi, Syed Amjah Ali Jaffri, Yasser Ebrahim, Hany Ibrahim, Akil Schedveda, Kenneth Scott, Philip Marcus, Hemnauth Mohabir, and Mohamed Maddy, who lived through hellish conditions at MDC and Passaic and came out the other side; your courage to stand up and tell the world what happened to you, and to expose the human toll of these oppressive policies, is a constant source of inspiration to all of us at CCR.

Introduction

Rachel Meeropol

I FIRST MET FAROUK ABDEL-MUHTI on February 5, 2003 in a dingy visiting cubicle at Passaic County Jail in Paterson, New Jersey. At that point, he had already spent ten months in immigration detention. He was arrested in April of 2002 on a seven-year-old deportation order as part of the increasingly aggressive and targeted enforcement of civil immigration laws in the wake of 9/11. Farouk was a stateless Palestinian; he was born in Ramallah in 1947 and moved to New York in the seventies. The FBI and the INS had nowhere to send him, so like so many other immigration detainees without a home country, Farouk was simply placed in detention.

In many ways, Farouk's story follows that of the other post-9/11 detainees chronicled in this book. He was kept in the same overcrowded and brutal jails and faced the same physical and verbal abuse as was documented on video and in a report by the Office of the Inspector General. Like other post-9/11 detainees, Farouk was beaten repeatedly, harassed by guards, and constantly moved between facilities in New York, New Jersey, and Pennsylvania. In other ways, he was different from many other prisoners—shortly after I met with him, he was put in solitary confinement for eight continuous months in an attempt to prevent him from organizing other detainees against their detention and its brutal conditions. Even within these extremely restrictive

11

surroundings, he still managed to educate and organize detainees *and* guards about social justice issues—such as reasons to oppose the U.S. war on Iraq.

Farouk was also different than most of the other noncitizens swept up in the U.S. government's aggressive post-9/11 policing in that he was eventually released and permitted to stay in the United States. In 2001, the Supreme Court ruled that if after six months in detention it is unlikely the government will successfully deport a person, that person must be released.[1] In April of 2004, upon the orders of a federal court judge relying on that precedent, the Department of Homeland Security's Bureau of Immigration and Customs Enforcement (ICE) finally released Farouk.

Three months after he was released from prison, Farouk addressed the Philadelphia Ethical Society on the issue of "Detentions and Torture: Building Resistance." Immediately after giving his speech, Farouk died. He used his last breaths for his people. Those who knew Farouk believe that by illegally holding him in immigration detention where he was beaten, harassed, and denied proper medical care for over two years, ICE compromised his health and perhaps sentenced him to an early death. Those of us who worked with him were deeply shocked by Farouk's death—perhaps this is because Farouk never took the time to complain about his own problems, he was too focused on those of others. Notes from our interviews with Farouk over the past few years document his countless references to the medical and legal needs of other detainees, but only passing reference to his own inability to obtain the high blood pressure medication he needed.

Why do I introduce this book by focusing on Farouk's story, one of so many? Because with this book, we hope not only to provide the reader with a historical, political, and legal analysis of executive detentions and abuse since 9/11 but also to share the stories of the individuals whose lives have been torn apart by these policies. After three years of challenging the Bush administration's actions in many forums, we at the Center for Constitutional Rights have come to know and care for clients in truly dire straits. Many of our clients are self-described "broken men" who remain unable to regain control of their lives and livelihood. Others inspire us by their courage, and their indomitable drive to continue to struggle for themselves and others.

In the wake of the torture scandal at Abu Ghraib, and the lawless detentions at Guantánamo, it is all too easy to overlook a case like Farouk's. Yet the two years that were stolen from him are irretrievable, and the tragedy of his early and perhaps avoidable death is a stark reminder of the human costs of the Bush administration's response to 9/11.

It is the goal of the authors and editor of this book to share with you as many stories as we can about these other victims of September 11, 2001. To do so, we have focused our analysis on five major issues related to post-9/11 detention: (1) the detentions of noncitizens as "enemy combatants" at Guantánamo Bay, Cuba; (2) the "rendition" or transfer of noncitizen prisoners under the direction or control of the United States; (3) the torture and abuse of prisoners in U.S. custody in Iraq, Afghanistan, and elsewhere; (4) the mass immigration sweeps conducted immediately after 9/11; and (5) the detention of citizen "enemy combatants" in the United States. Interspersed with the authors' analysis of the historical, legal, and practical significance of each form of detention and abuse you will find the detainees' own stories, in their own words. We have left these accounts completely intact except where it was necessary to edit for space, or where we were concerned that the individual's meaning might be unclear due to mistakes in spelling or grammar.

It is our goal with this collection to provide readers with an in-depth understanding of these extreme forms of illegal government action. However, it is equally important that readers understand the context in which these extreme forms of oppression have flourished. The Bush administration has reacted to the 9/11 attacks with policies, regulations, and rhetoric designed to scare the American public into accepting a full-fledged assault on civil liberties. This assault did not happen overnight; instead, the Bush administration built on oppressive laws and policies already in existence to consolidate executive and law enforcement power through an erosion of our civil rights, and a campaign of intimidation, isolation, and profiling aimed primarily at activists, noncitizens, and immigrants of color. The Bush administration's actions post-9/11 cannot be misunderstood as a spontaneous eruption of repressive policies; rather, they represent a long-planned and well-developed move toward authoritarian control.

With this introduction, we engage in a critical analysis of some of the domestic policies carried out by the Bush administration in the last three years, and can begin to trace parallels and draw conclusions about not only the moral bankruptcy of our government's actions but also the flawed policing and protection each such action represents.

THE USA PATRIOT ACT AND BEYOND[2]

No analysis of the Bush administration's attack on civil liberties post-9/11 could be complete without at least some discussion of the USA PATRIOT Act. Six weeks after the devastation of September 11, 2001, Congress passed the "Uniting and Strengthening America by Providing Appropriate Tools Required to Intercept and Obstruct Terrorism Act of 2001," more popularly known by its acronym, the USA PATRIOT Act. The name of the act and the speed with which it was forced through Congress were early indicators of the by now familiar tactics of the Bush administration: (1) taking advantage of every opening to consolidate power; and (2) equating criticism of their policies with support for terrorism.

The USA PATRIOT Act weighs in at 342 pages. It is the result of a wish list of law enforcement powers given to Congress by Attorney General John Ashcroft. Ashcroft insisted that Congress grant the Department of Justice these new powers within three days of submitting the proposal, and when they missed that deadline, he stated in public that Congress would be at fault if there was another terrorist attack while the bill was pending. It strains the imagination to think that Ashcroft's complex and far-reaching requests could have been conceived of and compiled in the hectic days after 9/11. Far more likely is that Ashcroft, with the approval of the Bush administration, had always planned to ask for powers like these—9/11 simply offered the perfect vehicle to articulate them and get them approved. These new powers are really just the cherry on the top of several decades of increasingly militant and aggressive policing of civilians.

The USA PATRIOT Act was passed by a Congress that had been evacuated from anthrax-contaminated offices and felt threatened by continuous alerts of more terrorist attacks. Few congresspeople actually read the act, there was little public debate or discussion, and not a single conference report or committee report was generated. The act passed the Senate by a vote of 98 to 1, Russ Feingold (D-WI) being the lone dissenter, and it passed the House 356 to 66. On October 26, 2001, it was signed into law.

The most problematic aspect of the USA PATRIOT Act is the severe intrusion of privacy it allows. The act accomplishes this in three ways: (1) by greatly expanding the intelligence and surveillance powers of the executive branch; (2) by limiting or removing judicial oversight of surveillance and investigation; and (3) by allowing for the increased sharing of information between criminal and intelligence agencies.[3]

The USA PATRIOT Act is not only about increased surveillance. It also has serious repercussions for political activists who engage in civil disobedience and direct action. Section 802 of the act expands the definition of the federal crime of terrorism to include "domestic terrorism," which is defined as "acts dangerous to human life that are a violation of the criminal laws" if they "appear intended to influence the policy of a government by intimidation or coercion" and take place, primarily, in the United States. The definition is so broad that it could allow prosecutors to target nonviolent direct action, including vandalism undertaken by radical environmentalists. In practice, it allows federal agents increased latitude to investigate and target dissident political groups.

The act also limits the rights of activists and academics who wish to host foreign speakers. Section 411 of the USA PATRIOT Act imposes an ideological litmus test for entry into the United States. Noncitizens who are members of groups that have endorsed terrorist activity in a way that has undermined U.S. efforts to fight terrorism, as determined by the secretary of state, are barred from entering the country. This provision is similar to the McCarran-Walter Act of 1952, which, before it was repealed in 1990, was used to exclude many prominent scholars, writers, and activists from entry into the United States, including Gabriel García Márquez and Pablo Neruda.

Not only activists are targeted. Like so many other government policies post-9/11, the USA PATRIOT Act unfairly targets and profiles noncitizens. Section 411 of the USA PATRIOT Act allows for the deportation of noncitizens based on participation in terrorist activity, defined as any crime that involves the use of a weapon or dangerous device other than for personal monetary gain. "Participation" can include fund raising, soliciting members, or providing "material support" to a "terrorist organization," even if that organization is engaged in humanitarian or other legitimate activities and the noncitizen in question has supported only those legitimate activities. Before the USA PATRIOT Act, "terrorist organizations" were those officially designated as such, and the designation was published in the *Federal Register*. Under the USA

PATRIOT Act, a "terrorist organization" can include any previously undesignated group composed of two or more individuals who engage in terrorist activities.[4]

Finally, Section 412 allows the INS to hold any noncitizen suspected of terrorism for up to seven days without bond and without charges, based merely on a certification by the attorney general that he has reasonable grounds to believe the individual is engaged in terrorist activities or activities that threaten national security. "Reasonable grounds" is a level of suspicion that defies exact definition, but it is roughly comparable to the level of suspicion that police officers must have to stop an individual on the street. It is far less than the "probable cause" that is required before the police can arrest a citizen.

The USA PATRIOT Act was sold to a Congress and a public eager to do anything necessary to stop terrorism. Yet despite Bush and Ashcroft's continued protestations to the contrary, these provisions are simply unnecessary for our safety. Past terrorism prosecutions provide some evidence that law enforcement already had the tools it needed to investigate and bring to justice suspected terrorists; conveniently for the Bush administration, the public has no way of knowing to what use these new provisions have been put.

Beyond being unnecessary, these new powers, carried out in secret without judicial oversight, will likely do more to expose us to terrorist attacks than to protect us. Judicial and media scrutiny of executive action is not only valuable to deter and uncover government excesses or invasions of civil liberties, but it is also essential to ensuring that the executive is doing an effective job. Assessing executive action requires concrete knowledge about what the government is doing to protect us from terrorism; we cannot simply sit back and trust that they are using their new powers in valuable or productive ways. The courts and the independent media need to play their traditional role of exposing executive actions to scrutiny so that we can accurately judge whether our government is truly protecting us.

If Bush and Ashcroft didn't need the USA PATRIOT Act, they most certainly don't need the so-called Patriot II, an expansion of the already outrageous powers provided by Patriot I. Rumors of a second installment of the USA PATRIOT Act have been floating around for quite a while, but there was such a public outcry after the initial leak that the Bush administration seems to have abandoned the hope of passing it as one act. Instead, many of the provisions that were found in Patriot II found their way into parts of other bills, such as the CLEAR Act and the Homeland Security Enhancement Act.

TARGETING ACTIVISTS

The Bush administration's targeting of activists goes far beyond the USA PATRIOT Act. An important part of keeping control over public opinion is discrediting alternative points of view, yet the powerful social justice movements that have sprung from global opposition to the war in Iraq and domestic opposition to the Bush administration's assault on civil liberties express our collective unwillingness to accept oppression, heightened militarization, and murder in the name of "national security." This challenge has not gone unnoticed. On December 6, 2001, Attorney General John Ashcroft proclaimed: "To those who scare peace-loving people with phantoms of lost liberty, my message is this: your tactics only aid terrorists, for they erode our national unity and diminish our resolve."[5] Unfortunately, beyond the rhetoric, Bush and Ashcroft have implemented some very real policies to realize this message, the most significant of which is the revitalization of COINTEL-PRO-era tactics and strategies, made possible through destruction of decades-old restrictions on FBI investigation of political activists.

Between 1956 and 1971, then director of the FBI, J. Edgar Hoover, implemented the now infamous COINTELPRO program. In those days surveillance was only the first step; the next step was the infiltration of activist organizations, and the disruption of their activities to discredit movement leaders and the movements themselves. When the public learned of these excesses through leaked papers to the press, they were outraged, and the result was a series of meaningful restrictions on the FBI's ability to investigate domestic political activity.[6]

Under these new standards the FBI could not initiate an investigation of a domestic political group without a reasonable indication that the group was involved in criminal activity. Ashcroft gutted those restrictions in the spring of 2002 to once again allow agents to monitor meetings and protests even if they have no reason to suspect criminal activity. Ashcroft claimed to need this power to fight international terrorism, despite the fact that the domestic restrictions never limited investigation of international terrorist organizations—such investigations could already be initiated without any indication of criminal activity. Moreover, under the old standards, any tie to a foreign group would bring an otherwise purely domestic organization under the looser international standard. Despite Ashcroft's claims, we now know that this power is being used not just to fight terrorism but to suppress critical speech and intimidate activists.

In December of 2003, a confidential FBI memo was leaked to the *New York Times* that detailed a national program of surveillance and investigation of antiwar activists undertaken by the FBI with the aid of local law enforcement agencies. Although purportedly about "violent anarchists" (the government's current favorite boogeymen, who are consistently invoked to scare people away from large demonstrations), the memo actually instructs law enforcement agencies to "be alert to . . . possible indicators of protest activities," including using the internet to recruit members and raise money prior to demonstrations, providing training on how to interact with police officers, communicating via cell phones during protests, videotaping the police, and other protected and lawful actions. The memo requests that local law enforcement report the fruits of their surveillance to the nearest Joint Terrorism Task Force (JTTF).

According the FBI's web page, Joint Terrorism Task Forces are teams of state and local law enforcement officers, FBI agents, and other federal agents and personnel who work shoulder-to-shoulder to investigate and prevent acts of terrorism. Today, there are 66 JTTFs, including one in each of the FBI's 56 main field offices and ten in smaller offices. More than 2,300 personnel work on these task forces nationwide. There is also a newly created National Joint Terrorism Task Force in Washington, D.C., which collects and disseminates information to and from 30 agencies, including intelligence, public safety, and federal, state, and local law enforcement.

In February of 2004, when the National Lawyers Guild chapter at Drake University was served with a subpoena to turn over records related to an antiwar conference, including the names of student leaders and conference attendees, it was a local sheriff assigned to the JTTF who served the papers. And when nonviolent antiwar groups in California, Michigan, and New Mexico discovered that they had been infiltrated by undercover officers who were taking part in their meetings and, in some cases, suggesting illegal actions, it turned out that several of those officers also served on their local JTTFs. Joint Terrorism Task Force cops at the direction of the Justice Department have begun investigating unsolved crimes from the 1960s, and we have received reports of such investigations from aging ex–Black Panthers and Black Liberation Army members who are once again hearing that same old knock on their door, this time for crimes allegedly committed almost forty years ago. Even old radicals already under the government's control have felt the burn of increased government oppression—political prisoner Sundiata Acoli, for example, has been in solitary confinement since September 11, 2001.

Of course, the equation of terrorism and political dissent did not originate with the Bush administration. In fact, "terrorism" has long been a buzzword to justify spying and infiltration of political activists and organizers. In the 1980s, organizers with the Committee in Solidarity with the People of El Salvador (CISPES) and antinuclear activists—who a few years earlier had been labeled "radicals," "agitators," or "activists"—were labeled "terrorist" and investigated by the new JTTF.[7] More recently, during preparation for protests against the 2000 Republican National Convention in Philadelphia, activist groups were infiltrated by Pennsylvania state police who posed as union members. The infiltrators, who went through civil disobedience and nonviolence trainings with the group, later helped facilitate the arrest of several activists. The undercover agents urged heightened illegal activity and physical confrontation with police—against the principles and agreements of the activists. These state police agents provocateurs were under the supervision of Pennsylvania governor Tom Ridge—now head of the Department of Homeland Security.

The impetus for local law enforcement to equate political dissent with terrorism is clear. Federal money for countering terrorism is currently distributed to local governments based on their assessment of the number of potential terrorist threats in their area. The more radical groups that local law enforcement feel a need to investigate, the more federal money they receive.

What all this adds up to is that we are once again living in very scary times. The Bush administration has gone beyond rhetorical demonization of activists and has actually started policing protestors with money ear-marked for fighting terrorism, and so far, the general public has not seemed to notice, or care. As this book goes to print, we are still dealing with the aftermath of the Republican

National Convention, during which protestors were once again denied a permit for the protest location of their choice. As a result, thousands were arrested without cause and held in outrageous conditions for long periods of time, presumably to keep them off the streets for the duration of the convention.

TARGETING IMMIGRANTS

Of course, even more than activists, the group that has born the brunt of the Bush administration's post-9/11 crackdown is immigrants and noncitizens of color. Bush's racial profiling and overly aggressive policing of noncitizens has torn families apart and in many urban areas, destroyed whole communities. In Midwood and Brighton Beach, Brooklyn, for example, the *New York Times* reported that in the two years after 9/11, the Pakistani community shrank from 120,000 to half that.[8] While the post-9/11 sweeps described in chapter 9 are perhaps the most startling and egregious example of the morally repugnant (and startlingly inefficient) policy of using immigration status as a proxy for potential terrorists, the sweeps are not the entire story.

After a decade of progress in combating racial profiling in criminal law enforcement, the events of 9/11 have led to a wholesale resurgence of discriminatory official policy. For example, on September 11, 2002, the Immigration and Naturalization Services (INS) initiated the National Security Entry/Exit Registration System (NSEERS), which required all male nonimmigrants over the age of 16 from designated countries to report to the INS to be questioned, fingerprinted, and photographed. Of the first 20 countries to be designated, all but one—North Korea—were Arab or Muslim. During the registration process, thousands of noncitizens were mistreated and detained unnecessarily, and now face deportation. In December of 2002, for example, the INS office in Los Angeles detained around 400 men—most of whom were Iranian or Iraqi exiles with minor visa violations—who went there voluntarily in order to register under NSEERS. These mass arrests led to many individuals becoming fearful of showing up to register, even when they had a valid immigration status. Ashcroft has failed to explain how a *voluntary* requirement, which alienates the very communities in which law enforcement officials most need to build trust, could possibly help locate terrorists.[9]

The INS (and later the Department of Homeland Security) responded to accusations of racial, ethnic, and religious profiling and discrimination by stating that it intended to eventually register all nonimmigrants. Instead, on December 1, 2003, the INS suspended yearly registration requirements amid massive public outcry against the discriminatory, haphazard, and intimidating way the program was being applied. Before the suspension went into effect, however, more than 82,000 men from twenty countries voluntarily came forward to comply with the time-consuming and invasive interviews, and more than 2,870 were detained for some period of time as a result.[10] Although most of NSEERS's requirements have been suspended, those individuals who complied with the discriminatory law and were thus placed into deportation proceedings have received no clemency. Indeed, at least 2,000 men from New York, and over 13,000 nationwide face deportation today.[11]

NSEERS was not the only new immigration requirement that blatantly relied on racial, religious, and national origin profiling. On December 5, 2001, the INS announced its new "Alien Absconder Apprehension Initiative," which provided the FBI with the names of 314,000 immigrants with outstanding deportation orders for inclusion in the National Crime Information Center database. The Department of Justice decided to initially focus on 6,000 of these individuals who came from countries with suspected ties to al Qaeda. Immigration violations are largely civil violations, not punishable by criminal law. Including such information on a criminal database means that a routine traffic stop can result in serious immigration consequences, and that police departments become responsible for enforcing the immigration laws.

Although racial profiling of noncitizens has become something of a pet project for the Bush administration, it is important to realize that many of the recent detentions and policies were made possible by racist immigration laws passed during the Clinton administration. In 1996, Congress passed and Clinton signed the Illegal Immigration Reform and Immigrant Responsibility Act, or IIRAIRA, which increased immigration officers' presence at borders and increased criminal penalties for immigration violations. The act allows, and in some cases requires, long-term detention of individuals who are awaiting a determination of their immigration status. The act expanded the definition of "aggravated felony" (crimes for which noncitizens can be deported) to include almost every felony, including things like shoplifting and other nonviolent, relatively minor offenses. Most of the noncitizens detained and deported under this harsh law before *and after* 9/11 were individuals of Caribbean and Latin American descent. The harshness with which these individuals are treated allows the Bush administration to brag of its get-tough policies and reassure the public of our impenetrable borders. There is no mention of the human toll, nor any way to quantify claimed increases in safety.

Examining the patterns of aggressive and discriminatory policing outlined above informs our understanding of the executive actions explored in the following pages. If the voluntary special registration program failed to ferret out terrorist immigrants, and the post-9/11 special-interest detentions resulted in many deportations but no terrorism charges, why should we believe that the Guantánamo detentions and brutal interrogations at Abu Ghraib were any more effectively designed or executed? Taken together, we can see that the Bush administration's post-9/11 crackdown on civil liberties is not a story of freedom sacrificed for security, but of freedom sacrificed for nothing, or at least nothing useful.

The deportations and detentions, alternately spun to the media as proof of our victories against terrorists or evidence of the continued threat, are nothing more than public relations stunts, purchased at a cost dear to the American people, and to people of color around the world.

NOTES

1 *Zadvydas v. Davis*, 533 U.S. 678 (2001).
2 For an extremely helpful reference on the USA PATRIOT Act, read Nancy Chang's *Silencing Political Dissent*, also available from Seven Stories Press.
3 For example, Section 213 of the USA PATRIOT Act authorizes federal agents to conduct "sneak and peak" searches. This means that a federal officer can get a warrant to search your home or office, and then carry out the search without telling you, outside of your presence. All the agent has to do to get this kind of warrant is provide minimal evidence that delayed notice of the search will be useful. Even more troubling is Section 215 of the USA PATRIOT Act, which authorizes the director of the FBI, or an agent he has designated, to apply for a court order requesting personal records or tangible items based on a written statement that the records are being sought in connection to an international terrorism investigation. Although the investigation must be related to international terrorism, the target of the Section 215 order does not have to be someone who is even a suspect in that investigation. In fact, the FBI doesn't have to show probable cause nor even reasonable grounds to believe that the person whose records it seeks is engaged in any criminal activity. Under these Section 215 orders, the FBI can get bank records, medical records, school records, library records, and much more. Moreover, the whole process occurs in secrecy. The librarian or doctor or bank officer who is served with a Section 215 order is prohibited from disclosing the fact to anyone else—this means that people whose records have been accessed may never know that their privacy has been invaded.
4 The Center for Constitutional Rights has successfully challenged several aspects of this provision in its suit, *Humanitarian Law Project v. Ashcroft*.
5 United States Attorney General John Ashcroft, testimony before the Senate Judiciary Committee, December 6, 2001.
6 *See* Ward Churchill and Jim Vander Wall, *The Cointelpro Papers: Documents for the FBI's Secret Wars Against Dissent in the United States* (South End Press, Cambridge, Mass.: 1990 and 2002), for a thorough analysis of COINTELPRO and its continued relevance.
7 Michelle Goldberg, "Outlawing Dissent," Salon.com, February 11, 2004.
8 Andrea Elliott, "In Brooklyn, 9/11 Damage Continues," *New York Times*, June 7, 2003, A9.
9 For more information on special registration, see *Special Registration: Discrimination and Xenophobia as Government Policy*, a report from the Asian American Legal Defense and Education Fund, January 2004.
10 Ibid.
11 Ibid.

1

Open Letter to President George W. Bush from Two Former Detainees

Shafiq Rasul and Asif Iqbal

Shafiq and Asif are two British citizens in their twenties. They were detained in Afghanistan in 2001 and turned over to U.S. military forces. The "Tipton boys," as they became known, spent over two years in detention at Guantánamo Bay, Cuba, before being released into British custody. They were never charged with a crime by British or American authorities and were released from British custody shortly after their release from Guantánamo.

DEAR SIR:

We were kept captive, unlawfully, by U.S. Forces in Guantánamo Bay for more than two years until the 8th March of this year [2004]. We are now back in the United Kingdom.

The legality of our detention was due to be considered by the Supreme Court when we were suddenly pulled out of Guantánamo Bay and taken to England, where we were released within 24 hours.

During the past week, we have seen with disgust the photographs of men detained and tortured in Iraq. At the same time we are reading with astonishment in the newspapers here, official statements made by the United States Government about *"interrogation techniques"* used at Guantánamo Bay that are completely untrue.

For instance, we read that these techniques *"are meant to wear down detainees but the rules forbid the kind of tortures coming to light in Iraq."* The techniques, it is said, are *"designed to cause disorientation, fatigue and stress,"* *"but there is no stripping detainees naked."* There is *"no physical contact at all . . . our procedures prohibit us from disrobing a prisoner for any reason at all"* (Army Colonel David McWilliams). It is said that *"more extreme methods such as near day long interrogations require superior authorisation and medical monitoring"* and that there is *"no stripping or humiliation or physical abuse at Camp Delta."*

Our own experience, and our close knowledge of the experience of other men detained beside us, demonstrates that each of these claims is completely untrue. From the moment of our arrival in Guantánamo Bay (and indeed from long before) we were deliberately humiliated and degraded by the use of methods that we now read U.S. officials denying.

At Kandahar, we were questioned by U.S. soldiers on our knees, in chains, with guns held to our heads, and we were kicked and beaten. They kept us in "three-piece suits" made up of a body belt with a chain down to leg irons and hand shackles attached. Before we boarded the plane to Guantánamo, they dressed us in earmuffs, painted-out goggles and surgical masks so we were completely disoriented. On the plane, they chained us to the floor without access to a toilet for the 22-hour flight.

Our interrogations in Guantánamo, too, were conducted with us chained to the floor for hours on end in circumstances so prolonged that it was practice to have plastic chairs for the interrogators that could be easily hosed off because prisoners would be forced to urinate during the course of them and were not allowed to go to the toilet. One practice that was introduced specifically under the regime of General Miller was "short shackling" where we were forced to squat without a chair with our hands chained between our legs and chained to the floor. If we fell over, the chains would cut into our hands. We would be left in this position for hours before an interrogation, during the interrogations (which could last as long as 12 hours), and sometimes for hours while the interrogators left the room. The air conditioning was turned up so high that within minutes we would be freezing. There was strobe lighting and loud music played that was itself a form of torture. Sometimes dogs were brought in to frighten us.

We were not fed all the time that we were there, and when we were returned to our cells, we would not be fed that day.

We should point out that there were—and no doubt still are—cameras everywhere in the interrogation areas. We are aware that evidence that could contradict what is being said officially is in existence. We know that CCTV[1] cameras, videotapes, and photographs exist since we were regularly filmed and photographed during interrogations and at other times, as well.

They recorded the interrogations in which we were driven to make false confessions: they insisted we were the other men in a video they showed us from August 2000 with Osama bin Laden and Mohamed Atta, but we had been in England at that time. After three months in solitary confinement under harsh conditions and repeated interrogations, we finally agreed to confess. Last September an agent from MI5 came to Guantánamo with documentary evidence that proved we could not have been in Afghanistan at the time the video was made. In the end we could prove our alibis, but we worry about people from countries where records are not as available.

Soldiers told us personally of going into cells and conducting beatings with metal bars which they did not report. Soldiers told us "we can do anything we want." We ourselves witnessed a number of brutal assaults upon prisoners. One, in April 2002, was of Jummah Al-Dousari from Bahrain, a man who had become psychiatrically disturbed, who was lying on the floor of his cage immediately near to us when a group of eight or nine guards known as the ERF Team (Extreme Reaction Force) entered his cage. We saw them severely assault him. They stamped on his neck, kicked him in the stomach even though he had metal rods there as a result of an operation, and they picked up his head and smashed his face into the floor. One female officer was ordered to go into the cell and kick him and beat him which she did, in his stomach. This is known as "ERFing." Another detainee, from Yemen, was beaten up so badly that we understand he is still in hospital eighteen months later. It was suggested that he was trying to commit suicide. This was not the case.

We wish to make it clear that all of these and other incidents and all of the brutality, humiliation, and degradation were clearly taking place as a result of official policies and orders.

Under the regime of General Miller, it was regular practice for detainees to have all of their hair including their beards shaved off. We were told that it was for failure to cooperate in interrogation (including if they said that you had failed a polygraph test). All of this would be filmed on video camera while it was happening. We understand that even in the face of representatives from the Red Cross having witnessed at least one such instance for themselves, the administration of the camp denied to the Red Cross that this practice existed.

Sometimes detainees would be taken to the interrogation room day after day and kept short-shackled without interrogation ever happening, sometimes for weeks on end. We received distressed reports from other detainees of their being taken to the interrogation room, left naked and chained to the floor, and of women being brought into the room who would inappropriately provoke and indeed molest them. It was completely clear to all the detainees that this was happening to particularly vulnerable prisoners, especially those who had come from the strictest of Islamic backgrounds.

Shortly before we left, a new practice was started. People would be taken to what was called the "Romeo" block where they would be stripped completely. After three days they would be given underwear. After another three days they would be given a top, and then after another three days given trouser bottoms. Some people only ever got underwear. This was said to be for "misbehaving." (Punishment within Guantánamo Bay was constantly imposed for the breaking of any camp "rule" including, for instance, having two plastic cups in your cage when you were only allowed to have one or having an extra prayer bead or too much toilet paper or excess salt.) So far as leaving detainees naked is concerned, it is our understanding that the Red Cross complained to the Colonel and then the General and after that to the U.S Administration itself about the practice.

We are completely sure that the International Red Cross has all of these complaints recorded and must undoubtedly have drawn all of them to the attention of the Administration. We therefore find it extraordinary that such lies are being told publicly today by senior officials as to the conditions and methods used at Guantánamo Bay. We are confident that records and pictures must exist and that these should all now be provided to the public in your country as well as ours at the earliest opportunity so that they can form their own judgement.

We look forward to an immediate response in view of the misinformation that is being put into the public domain worldwide and which we know to be untrue.

Yours sincerely,
Shafiq Rasul and Asif Iqbal

NOTE

1   Closed Circuit Television.

2

The Guantánamo Prisoners

Michael Ratner

IT HAS BEEN CALLED an "American Gulag," "A Lawless Human Warehouse," "A Legal Black Hole," "A Glimpse into Our Future," "A Cold Storage Facility," and the "First Offshore Concentration Camp of the Empire." The entire world knows it by these epithets: it is the United States prison camp at Guantánamo Bay, Cuba.

It is a prison—or rather a number of prisons—that as of this writing hold approximately 550 human beings from over 40 countries. Most of the detainees were captured, kidnapped, or arrested—oftentimes on the basis of unreliable information—during the U.S. military operations that have been occurring in Afghanistan since 9/11. Most of the detainees have been held incommunicado for more than two years. We do not know most of their names, as the United States will not give out this information. To date, only four have been charged with crimes.[1] Each detainee may have been interrogated as many as 200 times. Almost none have had access to an attorney,[2] or have had contact with their families. None have had access to any court or judicial process for asserting their innocence. They could be held forever. These are executive detentions totally outside both domestic and international law. The detainees are truly America's disappeared.

HOW IT ALL BEGAN: WHY GUANTÁNAMO?

In the late 1800s the United States intervened in the Cuban War of Independence against the Spanish, later known as the Spanish-American War. Ostensibly coming to the aid of the Cubans, the United States ultimately took control of Cuba at the end of the war. As one of the conditions for granting "independence" to Cuba, the United States insisted on what amounts to a perpetual lease on approximately thirty-one square miles of land on a southeast portion of the island—an area larger then Manhattan. This is the U.S. naval base at Guantánamo Bay. The lease gives the United States "complete jurisdiction and control" over the area and it continues in perpetuity unless *both* countries agree to end the arrangement.

Despite claims of national sovereignty made by Cuba over the area, the United States insists its occupation is legal and that it will remain in Guantánamo until it decides otherwise. The U.S. naval web site accurately describes Guantánamo Bay as "a Naval reservation, which for all practical purposes is American territory."[3] This is unlike any other base the United States has in a foreign country. The United States is essentially sovereign over Guantánamo. Cuba and its courts have no authority over the base in any respect.

The naval base is self-sufficient, with approximately 7,000 military and civilian residents—an American enclave with all the residential, commercial, and recreational trappings of a small U.S. city. It has its own schools, generates its own power, provides its own internal transportation, supplies its own water, and has an airfield. Crimes committed by either civilians or foreign nationals living on the base are brought before courts in the mainland United States.

Over the years Guantánamo has been used for a number of different purposes. Initially, and according to the lease, the base was to be used solely as a "coaling station" for refueling ships.

However, for many years the United States has acted outside the limits of the lease, in reliance on the fact that there is nothing Cuba, or anyone else, can do about it.

Prior to the detentions resulting from the post-9/11 "war on terrorism," Guantánamo Bay was used as a detention camp for Haitians and Cubans seeking refuge in the United States, which included the world's first camp for HIV-positive refugees. In 1990, during the administration of Bush I, President Aristide was overthrown in Haiti and the ensuing bloodbath led thousands to flee. The United States did not want these Haitian refugees coming to the United States and decided to hold them at Guantánamo. These detentions set the precedent for the post-9/11 detentions and demonstrate that using the base as a zone outside the law was not the brainchild of the Bush II administration.

Apart from its physical location near Haiti in the Caribbean, Guantánamo provided many advantages to the United States. It is remote—off-limits to reporters and relatives of servicemen—and can only be visited with the permission of the U.S. government. However, it is still close enough to the United States for soldiers and officials to shuttle back and forth to the mainland with ease. Most important, it has been treated by the United States as a law-free zone. That is to say, the Bush I administration, the Clinton administration, and the Bush II administration have all operated as if no court in the world could hear a case brought on behalf of a Guantánamo refugee or detainee. In effect this meant that the U.S. government could treat refugees and detainees however it wished; it could beat them, punish them, detain them forever or send them back to their oppressors in Haiti, and there was nothing anyone could do about it.

This claim regarding the Haitians was soon tested by lawyers who brought suit in U.S. courts on behalf of refugees in danger of being sent back to Haiti and on behalf of HIV refugees seeking release from the camp. The cases were bitterly contested by the government and they ultimately resulted in conflicting court decisions on whether or not judges could hear claims by people held at Guantánamo. To the extent those courts concluded that the naval base at Guantánamo was akin to United States sovereign territory, they permitted judicial review and determined that the refugees had some constitutional protection.[4] To these courts Guantánamo is effectively American territory, much like Puerto Rico or the Canal Zone.

Other courts, however, found Guantánamo more akin to a foreign country and used this theory to deny the refugees any right to judicial review or constitutional protection.[5] The Supreme Court itself never addressed the status of Guantánamo prior to June 28, 2004, when it decided that courts in the United States could hear cases brought on behalf of those detained at Guantánamo.[6]

The status of Guantánamo, which for all intents and purposes is U.S.-controlled territory, made this result almost unavoidable. Logically, it is simply impossible to accept the argument that what occurs there should be exempt from U.S. court review. It is also difficult to accept the view that the United States can imprison people anywhere in the world, even in a foreign country, and be free from judicial oversight. If judicial oversight depended on the location of a given prison, the United States could evade oversight simply by moving someone. The Supreme Court's June 2004 decision directly prohibits such a notion and establishes that Guantánamo detainees *do* have rights, and that they have the opportunity to argue for their release in federal court.

WHO ARE THE GUANTÁNAMO DETAINEES?

On October 7, 2001, the United States and its allies, including the Afghan Northern Alliance, launched a war against the Taliban rulers of Afghanistan and al Qaeda members who were present there. The attack quickly forced the Taliban from power, and in the immediate aftermath thousands of alleged Taliban and al Qaeda fighters were captured, many of whom were detained under appalling conditions at prisons in Mazar-e Sharif and Shibarghan.[7] The Northern Alliance forces—which captured many of these prisoners—later freed some of them; others continue to be imprisoned in Afghanistan.[8] A number of prisoners were also held in Bagram, Afghanistan, a U.S. detention facility where abuse and torture of prisoners is reportedly commonplace.[9]

On January 11, 2002, the U.S. military began transporting some of the prisoners captured in Afghanistan to Camp X-Ray at Guantánamo Bay. Camp X-Ray was located on an isolated part of the naval base, which itself is located on a remote part of Cuba. The name Camp X-Ray, although probably a sick joke, accurately described the camp; the wire cages in which detainees were held (with the lights blazing 24 hours a day) enabled guards to see prisoners at all times.

There have been reliable allegations of ill-treatment of prisoners in transit to Guantánamo, including reports that they were shackled to the floor in the plane, hooded, and sedated during the 25-hour flight from Afghanistan, and that their beards and heads were forcibly shaved.

Over the next months, more prisoners were taken to Camp X-Ray. It is assumed that most of the detainees were allegedly associated with the Taliban or al Qaeda and taken from Afghanistan or Pakistan, although it is debatable whether or not civilians arrested in Pakistan were taken from the "theater of war."[10] However, prisoners from other places are also imprisoned in Guantánamo, including five Algerians, three from The Gambia, and a Yemeni from Bosnia.[11] These detentions indicate that Guantánamo is being used for more than just those picked up in Afghanistan and Pakistan, and will be used to detain others that U.S. officials suspect are dangerous, might have valuable information, or are somehow involved in terrorism.

The fact that the government is using Guantánamo for prisoners other then those detained during wartime is especially frightening. The United States is acting as an international roving police force, kidnapping whom it chooses, ignoring extradition laws, and taking those it detains to Guantánamo and other detention facilities. This approach is patently illegal; if those it detains are suspected of crimes, then they must be charged and tried as such and not taken to detention camps and held indefinitely.

In late April 2002, the United States transferred its Camp X-Ray prisoners to a new longer-term prison camp that was designed to house as many as 2,000 prisoners—Camp Delta.[12] With the opening of Camp Delta, Camp X-Ray closed the same month. Although Camp Delta was built to better protect prisoners from the elements, its layout, like Camp X-Ray's, enables the military to observe the detainees, whether in or out of their cells, at all times.

WHAT WE KNOW ABOUT THE DETAINEES

Not much is known about those imprisoned in Guantánamo; certainly, nothing is known publicly as to what crimes—if any—individual detainees are suspected of having committed. Because so little is known, it is impossible to verify the government's claims regarding their dangerousness or commitment to terrorism, or to know if any are there by mistake. Few attorneys, and no family or press are allowed to speak with the detainees, but the International Committee of the Red Cross has a regular presence in Guantánamo and presumably has visited the prison and the detainees. Allegedly the Red Cross has written a number of reports to U.S. officials criticizing the conditions at Guantánamo and the interrogation techniques used there. However, those reports have not been made public, and as is standard with the Red Cross, it has said nothing regarding the condition of individual detainees.

The U.S. administration has made public statements regarding the alleged character of those detained, without allowing any of the detainees access to attorneys to help them refute these claims. At the time of the transfers to Guantánamo, Secretary of Defense Donald Rumsfeld called the detainees "hardened criminals willing to kill themselves and others for their cause."[13] Emphasizing their dangerousness, he said, "Every time people have messed with these folks, they've gotten in trouble. And they are very well trained. They're willing to give up their lives, in many instances."[14] The U.S. military officials in charge of the prison said they were told to expect "the worst of the worst." "These are the worst of a very bad lot," said Vice President Cheney. "They are very dangerous."[15]

There may well be terrorists among those imprisoned. However, until the Supreme Court forced it to do so in June 2004, the United States failed to bring anyone before any kind of tribunal or court to determine who is a terrorist, who is a prisoner of war, and who is an innocent civilian. On July 30, 2004, the first tribunals opened for business, and on August 13, 2004, they issued their first rulings. "Lawyers for some of the detainees," reported the *New York Times* following the first rulings, "said the tribunals, known formally as Combatant Status Review Tribunals, did not comply with the rulings of the Supreme Court in June requiring that people held as unlawful enemy combatants be able to challenge their detentions in a fair proceeding with due process protections. . . . Lawyers for the detainees say federal court is the proper forum for adjudicating their rights."[16]

Critics of the Guantánamo tribunals say they do not satisfy the Supreme Court's requirements. Detainees, according to the July order establishing the tribunals, are provided with military officers, not lawyers, to act as their "personal representatives"; the representatives may review only "reasonably available information"; the detainee may call only "reasonably available witnesses"; the tribunals are made up of "three neutral commissioned officers of the

U.S. Armed Forces," not independent judges, and the rules of evidence do not apply.[17]

The detainees who went through the first four tribunals were held to be properly designated as "enemy combatants" and according to these tribunals may be held indefinitely.

Despite these rulings however, and based on information from the hundreds of persons who have been released so far, it appears that the United States is exaggerating by portraying many of those at Guantánamo as terrorists. These releases, sometimes after over two years in Guantánamo, demonstrate that the administration's sweeping rhetoric has been overblown. If these men are some of the "worst of the worst," how come many were never charged with any crime, by any country? And why did it take so long to determine that they were not terrorists?

In May 2003, after over a year at Guantánamo, the Bush administration freed prisoner number 671, Abassin Sayed.[18] After his release, a reporter found him in Afghanistan driving his taxi and playing Hindi music on his radio. Sayed's story reveals a lot about those still imprisoned at Guantánamo.

In April 2002 Sayed was driving his taxi when a gang of local Afghans stopped him at a checkpoint. American soldiers were being ambushed in the area and wanted to capture those responsible. The local Afghans were only too glad to help out, even if those stopped were not involved in the attacks. Although he protested that he was only a taxi driver, Abassin Sayed was turned over to the Americans.

Abassin Sayed never had a chance to prove that he was innocent and was never given any legal process. He was taken to the U.S. airbase at Bagram, Afghanistan, spent a month in an Afghan jail, and then was flown to Guantánamo, where he arrived tied, gagged, masked, and outfitted with dark goggles. He said of his arrival, "It was the act of an animal to treat a human being like that. It was the worst day of my life." He was put into a small cell with the lights on 24 hours a day. As he said, "The lights were so strong, you couldn't differentiate between day and night. If you tried to cover your face to sleep, the soldiers came in and told you not to do that."[19]

When Sayed was found exercising in his cell, he was punished with five days of solitary confinement and was denied blankets and other basic amenities. He was interrogated eleven times for six or seven hours at a time. He was punished in a similar fashion for being unable to answer questions during interrogation. And yet, Sayed's treatment was by no means the most severe; other prisoners are reported to have been interrogated over one hundred times.

Abassin Sayed's best friend, also a taxi driver, is still detained in Guantánamo. His crime? He had asked what had happened to his friend Abassin Sayed after he had been arrested; just for asking, he too was arrested, turned over to the United States, and shipped off to Guantánamo.

Abassin Sayed's case is not unique. The U.S. military dropped leaflets in Afghanistan offering large sums of money for information leading to the capture of terrorists. Many apparently took up the offer and turned in innocent civilians for their bounty. A military interrogator at Camp Delta estimates that as many as 20 percent of the men in captivity at Guantánamo are innocent.[20] Dozens of prisoners—if not more—are described in U.S. intelligence reports as farmers, taxi drivers, laborers, and shoemakers.[21] According to these reports, at least 59 individuals from Afghanistan and Pakistan were captured and shipped off to Guantánamo despite not fitting the screening criteria for such a transfer.[22] As one military official who served as an interrogator observed, "If they weren't terrorists before, they certainly could be now."[23]

In October 2002 three Afghani men were released after spending almost one year in captivity at Guantánamo. One of the released men reported that he was 105 years old. *New York Times* reporter David Rhode described him in the following manner: "Babbling at times like a child, the partially deaf, shriveled old man was unable to answer the simplest questions."[24] When asked if he was angry with American soldiers, he said that he did not mind, because they "took my old clothes and gave me new clothes." A second Afghani man, released at the same time, said that he was 90 years old and was described as a "wizened old man with a cane" who had been arrested in a raid on his village.[25]

A third, younger man said that he had been cut off from the outside world for eleven months and had only received a letter from his family three days before he was to leave Guantánamo.[26] He said that he was confined to his cell 24 hours a day with only two 15-minute breaks for exercise a week. This third man admitted that he had fought with the Taliban, but said that he had been forced to do so. After he surrendered, he said, soldiers of the warlord Abdul Rashid Dostum falsely told the United States that he and nine others were Taliban officials. His release appears to confirm the essential elements of his story. These men are hardly the "worst of the worst." Here were men who should have never been taken to Guantánamo. Here were men who, had there been a fair hearing before some form of a tribunal, would have been freed long ago.

Two other men were freed from Guantánamo in early 2004—Asif Iqbal and Shafiq Rasul. They were from Tipton, England, and had initially traveled to Pakistan prior to 9/11 for the purpose of a marriage arranged by Iqbal's parents. This author met with them in England shortly after their release and was stunned by their story. They are presently 22 years old, which means they were picked up when they were 20. At the time of the meeting they were quite open about discussing the horrors they had undergone. They had been captured by a warlord of the Northern Alliance and had almost died when they were imprisoned in sweltering shipping containers in Afghanistan (fewer than 30 of the 300 imprisoned in the container survived) before being turned over to the Americans, presumably for money. In Afghanistan they were treated brutally by American forces and eventually shipped off to Guantánamo. They describe the abuse and torture they suffered there in chapter 1, and in a 115-page personal report available on the Center for Constitutional Right's web site.[27]

Iqbal and Rasul's case illustrates not only the brutality of Guantánamo but also the unreliable nature of information gained by coercive interrogation techniques. U.S. interrogation officers showed the two a video of Osama bin Laden and claimed that two of the young men in the video were Iqbal and Rasul. They denied it, indicated that they were in the UK at the time and offered to prove it, and pointed out that the men did not look like them. The interrogator refused to believe them, used coercive measures, and after three months the young men "confessed" that it was them in the video.

By this time a real movement against the Guantánamo detentions began emerging in the UK. Eventually British intelligence, MI5, proved to the United States that Iqbal and Raul were in the UK at the time the video was made, and that it could not have been them in the video. There are a lot of lessons here: One of the most important is that coercion begets false confessions and destroys people's lives. Another is that Iqbal and Rasul should never have been sent to Guantánamo—a hearing might have resolved their case a lot earlier.

Information about other detainees is also available through their families, as well as from delegations of foreign officials who have been permitted to visit. Some prisoners have been able to send short, censored letters to their families through the Red Cross. These letters are few and far between. A few families that have received letters have contacted lawyers and have asked them to file lawsuits on their sons' behalf. As a result, further information has emerged about the detainees.

For example, according to his family, Australian citizen Mamdouh Habib traveled to Pakistan in August 2001 to look for work and for a school for his two teenage sons. On October 5, 2002—just before he was about to return to Australia and two days before the United States attacked Afghanistan—he was detained by Pakistani officials. He was transported to Egypt, held there for a period of time, apparently tortured, and eventually turned over to the United States and imprisoned at Guantánamo. Obviously, he was nowhere near the fighting in Afghanistan.

Similarly, a delegation from Pakistan that visited Guantánamo concluded that almost all of the 58 Pakistanis detained were low-level foot soldiers and had no link to al Qaeda. Some of these men may have been imprisoned because of the bounty offered for capturing members of al Qaeda and the Taliban. After the delegation's visit, Pakistan requested the release of nearly all of the Pakistani prisoners. The request was granted in September 2004.

Amazingly, it is not only adults who are imprisoned in Guantánamo. Children are there as well. The current number is unknown, but in early 2004 three minors between 13 and 15 years old were freed. The International Committee of the Red Cross issued a statement shortly thereafter stating that Guantánamo was an inappropriate place to detain juveniles and that their detention posed a grave risk to their well-being. Detentions of juveniles at Guantánamo also violates the Optional Protocol to the Convention on the Rights of Children, which requires governments to rehabilitate former children soldiers (assuming this is what the captured children are). As Human Rights Watch has said, "Rehabilitation does not happen at Guantánamo."[28] International law establishes the right of families to maintain contact with their children, the right to a speedy determination of their children's cases, and that detention only be used as a last resort. It appears that the United States has violated—and is violating—each of these rights and requirements. In response to pressure from human rights groups, the United States now imprisons most children at a separate detention facility called Camp Iguana, but children 16 years and older continue to be held captive with the adult detainees at Camp Delta.

These stories of the innocent, of detainees not involved in any fighting, of detainees who were no more than foot soldiers, and of young children, demonstrate the importance of a legal process for determining the status of those imprisoned at Guantánamo, and of the callousness and inhumanity with which the United States is running its lawless prison camp.

CONDITIONS OF DETENTION

This author has had some personal experience with the living conditions at Guantánamo. In the early 1990s, I represented Haitian refugees who were held there and visited the base where they were held on numerous occasions; it is on that site that Camp Delta was later built. I later described the landscape there as "bleak and hardscrabble; little grows except cacti; the heat is intense, and scorpions, mosquitoes, and banana rats are abundant. It is out of the ninth circle of Dante's Hell. For 14 months, the refugees have used portable toilets that are rarely cleaned, that are filled with feces and urine. The camp is…[comprised of] temporary wooden barracks on concrete slabs. Within those 'homes,' 15 to 20 Haitians are huddled with only sheets hanging from the rafters. Rain, vermin, and rats are other occupants."[29]

If the United States treats innocent refugees in such a manner, imagine how they treat people they believe to be terrorists—"the worst of the worst." When the first wave of detainees arrived at Guantánamo, the environment was much the same, but the conditions of detention were far harsher. Initially, they were housed in makeshift, small (8 feet by 8 feet), open air, wire cages that failed to protect against the elements. The cages were surrounded by fences topped with barbed razor wire, and the compound was encircled with watchtowers. In this early period, the detainees remained shackled when using the portable toilets or showers, and temperatures frequently went above 95 degrees Fahrenheit. Halogen floodlights blazed into the cages all night. The first photographs of Camp X-Ray detainees released in January 2002 show shackled men kneeling in awkward positions wearing orange jumpsuits, blackened goggles, masks, and ear covers. The release of the photos caused an immediate public outcry against U.S. management of the prisoners.

Camp Delta, the longer-term prison camp, is apparently divided into five camps, two of which hold the vast majority of the detainees: the main camp no. 3, and a smaller camp no. 1, reserved for prisoners who cooperate. In the few photographs that have been released, Camp Delta looks like rows of one-story, self-storage facilities. The cells for the majority of the detainees are 8 feet by 6.75 feet, but they do have running water and apparently better protect the prisoners from sun and rain. Each cell holds one prisoner. The toilet is a hole in the floor. David Rose, a *Vanity Fair* reporter who visited Camp Delta in October of 2003, described a cell as a "faded green metal box a little larger than a king-size mattress." Three of the cells' four walls are made from see-through chain-links to enable the guards—some of whom are women—to have unfettered view of inmates at all times, even when they are using the bathroom. Guards pass the cells two times every minute.

Detainees who cooperate receive better treatment. Instead of being kept isolated, one per cell, the cooperators are permitted to live in a separate wing where they are grouped ten to a dormitory-type room. In addition, detainees who cooperate are rewarded with more exercise, a wider variety of food (including dates and McDonald's from the base restaurant), thicker mattresses, and access to books. Cooperators trade in their bright orange jumpsuits and are issued white ones in their place.

The military and the Bush administration brag that the food and medical treatment at Guantánamo are good, and that the prisoners are treated humanely. This is a lie. Evidence that has emerged since April 2004 demonstrates that prisoners are not treated humanely and that prisoners' serious medical conditions are used as tools of coercion. Testimonies from the "Tipton Three"[30] document that the United States has used coercion amounting to torture against detainees at Guantánamo. Such tactics have included dogs, stripping, sleep deprivation, stress positions, noise, starvation, and probably worse.

When all the circumstances are weighed, it is clear that Guantánamo has but one major purpose: to break prisoners' spirits to facilitate interrogation. Before learning of many of these stories, in February 2003, this author wrote the following sentence about treatment at Guantánamo: "At Guantánamo [interrogation] may not be done with physical torture or coercion, but it is nonetheless, mental torture." I now realize how naive and wrong I was.

Even prior to recent revelations about coercive methods of interrogation, it was already clear that the conditions of imprisonment at Guantánamo were inhuman. We have already noted the size and nature of the cells. Prisoners are isolated and not allowed to speak to other prisoners or guards. If they are deemed uncooperative, as are the majority, they are permitted to exercise for only 15 minutes twice a week, and permitted to shower just twice a week; both activities are undertaken while they are shackled at the hands and legs.

As detainee Moazzam Begg wrote to his parents in one of the few, heavily censored, letters they received from him through the Red Cross, "Boredom here is extreme. I have not seen the sun for over seven months except once for around two minutes." Begg also described the camel spider, the only 10-legged spider in the world. He said, "It moves like a race car and has a bite that causes flesh to decay—if left untreated . . . and in the summer there were plenty here, running into the cells and clambering over people. . . . Thank God it's winter!"[31]

The difficult physical conditions at Guantánamo, coupled with coercive interrogation techniques, clearly constitute cruel, inhuman, and degrading treatment, as well as torture, and are all flatly illegal under the Geneva Conventions and the Convention Against Torture.

Another grave aspect of the detentions is the desperation and hopelessness felt by detainees who have no rights and no idea what will to happen to them. As a result of these horrendous conditions, there were over 30 suicide attempts in the first two years, and as many as one-third of the detainees are on antidepressants. Allegedly there have been fewer suicide attempts in 2004. However, this appears to be because the U.S. military, in Orwellian fashion, has redefined such attempts as "manipulative self-injurious behavior."

In November 2002, the Red Cross denounced the way that the United States was operating Guantánamo—the indefinite detentions, the failure to tell the prisoners about their futures, and the use of the base as an interrogation camp. Christopher Girod, the senior Red Cross official in Washington, said, "One cannot keep these detainees in this pattern, this situation, indefinitely." He stated that it was intolerable that Guantánamo was used as "an investigation center, not a detention center . . . and that the open-endedness of the situation and its impact on the mental health of the population has become a major problem." Mr. Girod said that detainees regularly ask what is going to happen to them. "It's always the number one question," he said. "They don't know about the future."[32] He explained that he was speaking out because the United States failed to heed the Red Cross's prior private communications to the U.S. government.

When asked about the International Red Cross's criticism, Scott McClellan, then White House press secretary, responded,

"Let us remember these individuals are enemy combatants. These individuals are terrorists, or supporters of terrorists, and we were at war with terrorism. And the reason for detaining enemy combatants in the first place during a war is to gather intelligence, is to make sure these enemy combatants do not return to help our enemies plot attacks, or carry out attacks on the United States."[33]

In effect, this statement indicates the White House's belief that all the prisoners at Guantánamo are guilty and can thus be treated inhumanely. As of July 2004, none of the men imprisoned at Guantánamo were provided an opportunity to defend their innocence through any form of legal proceeding. The United States assumes them to be guilty despite the fact that many of those released are clearly not. There has been no apology to those who have lost years of their lives languishing in Guantánamo's cages. Even if some are one day found guilty of crimes, does that permit the U.S. military to assume guilt and strip people of fundamental rights—rights enshrined in law for hundreds of years?

WHAT RIGHTS SHOULD THE DETAINEES HAVE?

As far as we know, most of the detainees now at Camp Delta were alleged Taliban fighters and militia captured in Afghanistan. Humanitarian law, embodied primarily in the Geneva Conventions of 1949, provides a framework to determine the status of the alleged "enemy combatants."

The Geneva Conventions do not apply to the detainees captured outside the theater of war and alleged to be terrorists, such as those Guantánamo detainees arrested in Bosnia-Herzegovina or The Gambia. Those detainees are not soldiers and are not subject to military or humanitarian law. Instead, international human rights law or U.S. criminal law determines their rights. Each of them, alleged international terrorists included, must be formally charged, given access to counsel, and tried.

No matter what a person's status, international legal norms apply to every person detained. No one can be arbitrarily detained or dealt with outside the law.

The Bush administration did not apply the terms of the Conventions to any of the Guantánamo prisoners. Specifically, the United States refused to apply Article 4 of the Third Geneva Convention that requires that all regular members of a government's army be granted POW status, and that members of a militia fighting alongside those armed forces (potentially including members of al Qaeda captured on the battlefield) also receive such status. By refusing to apply this key provision, the Bush administration has in fact refused to apply the Geneva Conventions in a meaningful way.

Moreover, the U.S. decision that neither the Taliban fighters nor the militia fighting alongside them were POWs was made without following the procedures specified in Article 5 of the Third Geneva Convention. That article requires the convening of a "competent tribunal" to determine the status of each individual captured "should any doubt arise" as to his status. (Such "competent tribunals" are not the military commissions that the United States is establishing to try war crimes.) The Third Geneva Convention requires that all such prisoners be treated as POWs pending such hearings. The United States never held such "competent tribunals," but instead made a blanket determination that no one captured on the battlefield was a POW. The United States has repeatedly refused the entreaties of the international community to treat all the detainees under the Article 4 and 5 procedures established under the Third Convention.[34]

There has never been a valid reason for the United States not to employ tribunals. Prior to attacking Afghanistan, the U.S. military adopted regulations for these tribunals, which are staffed entirely by its military personnel. Tribunals were used in Vietnam, and over a thousand such tribunal hearings were held during the

1991 war against Iraq. Had such tribunals been held after the United States attacked Afghanistan, they could have identified early on who among those imprisoned at Guantánamo were wrongly detained. As to the others, many of them may have been found to be POWs with rights and protections afforded to them under the Geneva Conventions.

The United States has tried to justify its position legally, but its claims have no merit. It has labeled those detained as "enemy combatants" and asserts that the military's authority to capture and detain such individuals is well settled. But an "enemy combatant" is a general category, not a status under the Geneva Conventions or any other body of law. Under the Geneva Conventions, enemy combatants are either prisoners of war with all of the rights granted by that status or they are not, in which case they come under the protections of the Fourth Geneva Convention. The Fourth Convention treats such non-POWs as civilians, but if the person is suspected of activities hostile to the state, he can be detained and denied certain rights, such as the right to write letters. However, determinations as to a prisoner's status must be made individually, prisoner by prisoner. Importantly, anyone captured, POW or otherwise, can still be criminally prosecuted for war crimes or acts of terrorism.

By failing to adhere to the Geneva Conventions and treat those captured in Afghanistan as POWS, and by failing to determine the status of those captured on an individual basis, the United States has violated international humanitarian law. Its position raises serious questions as to the legal authority under which the Guantánamo detainees are being held. If, as the United States claims, the detainees have no status under the Geneva Conventions, then the rules of international human rights law apply. However, those rules require that the detainees be arrested, charged, represented by attorneys, and tried. Obviously this is not occurring; instead the United States is holding these people outside both international and domestic law.

The Geneva Conventions were created to provide, among other things, humane conditions for all detainees and prohibit "outrages upon personal dignity; torture or inhuman treatment; willfully causing great suffering; [and] causing serious injury to body or health." The United States has made violations of these prohibitions criminal in the War Crimes Act (18 U.S.C. § 2441), which provides substantial jail sentences—including the death penalty—for those convicted of war crimes.

The importance of these provisions of the Conventions and U.S. criminal law should not be underestimated in evaluating U.S. conduct in Guantánamo. A memo from Alberto R. Gonzales (the president's counsel) to the president on January 25, 2002, and leaked from the Bush administration, gives what appears to be the real explanation for why the president decided not to apply the Geneva Conventions to the Guantánamo detainees.

The memorandum to the president, written a few weeks after the United States sent the first detainees to Guantánamo, advises *not* to apply the Conventions. After engaging in some legal analysis, Gonzales points out that one of the important advantages to be gained by refusing to apply the Geneva Conventions is that the United States can then argue that the U.S. war crimes statute does not apply to the conduct of the administration in Guantánamo. This "substantially reduces the threat of domestic criminal prosecution under the War Crimes Act." Gonzalez continues by noting that "it is difficult to predict the motives of prosecutors and independent counsel who may in the future decide to pursue unwarranted charges based on Section 2241 [the War Crimes Statute]." Not applying the Geneva Conventions "would provide a solid defense to any future prosecution."[35]

This means that the Bush administration, up to and including the president, had apparently already decided to treat the Guantánamo detainees inhumanely. They had already decided to use coercive interrogation techniques that were criminal under

U.S. law, and they were afraid of criminal prosecution. They needed a legal defense, so they decided not to apply the Conventions.

It is unlikely that this would be a valid defense if a prosecutor ever got the courage to go after administration officials. The Conventions are the law of the United States; the president cannot simply dispense with them, and it is unlikely that his attempt to do so would be recognized by a court.

The Geneva Conventions also set limits on the duration of confinement. POWs may only be detained until the "cessation of active hostilities." Arguably, that has already occurred with regard to the war in Afghanistan. As to non-POWs, they may be held until the "general close of military operations," which arguably has also occurred in Afghanistan.

U.S. officials have stated that many of those held at Guantánamo will be held indefinitely.[36] According to Secretary of Defense Rumsfeld, this means until the "war on terrorism" is over, which could be many years; that is, until "we feel that there are not effective global terrorist networks functioning in the world…."[37] Regarding military commissions, Rumsfeld has said that even if such commissions acquit some detainees, they may still be detained on the base. In other words, the administration considers itself entitled to capture, arrest, and detain people from anywhere in the world, interrogate them, refuse them access to lawyers and family, not charge them or bring them before any courts, not release them even if tried and acquitted, and imprison them indefinitely, year after year.

INTERNATIONAL LEGAL CHALLENGES: EARLY VICTORIES

A month after the detentions at Guantánamo began, the Center for Constitutional Rights and various human rights groups successfully challenged the detentions before the Inter-American Commission on Human Rights of the Organization of American States (OAS).

While the Commission is not a court, its mission is to enforce the principal regional human rights treaty, the American Declaration of the Rights and Duties of Man, the provisions of which protect the right to life, fair trial, due process, and freedom from arbitrary detention. In its decision of March 13, 2002, the Commission urged the United States to "take the urgent measures necessary to have the legal status of the detainees at Guantánamo Bay determined by a competent tribunal."[38] The Commission explained that everyone who is captured by a state must have a legal status, and that it is for a tribunal, not a government, to determine that status. In strong language the Commission found that

> the detainees remain entirely at the unfettered discretion of the United States government. Absent clarification of the legal status of the detainees, the Commission considers that the rights and protections to which they might be entitled under international or domestic law cannot be said to be the subject of effective legal protection by the state.[39]

Although the Commission has ruled that member states of the OAS are under an "international legal obligation" to comply with its decisions, the United States has refused to do so. The Commission reiterated its order mandating tribunals in July 2002 and held a hearing on the failure of the United States to implement this ruling. The United States has still not complied, and there is no power in the Commission to compel compliance.

Another challenge to the detentions was filed in the courts of the UK on behalf of one of the detainees, Ali Abbasi, a British citizen. Although the British Court could not order a remedy for the detentions because the U.S. government was not a party to the lawsuit, it described the detention situation in stark terms: "[I]n apparent contravention of fundamental principles recognized in both jurisdictions [U.S. and UK] and by international law, Mr. Abbasi is at present arbitrarily detained in a 'legal black hole.'"[40] The Court was especially critical of the U.S. government's claim that there was no court in the United States that could review the indefinite detentions in a territory over which the United States has exclusive control. It hoped that the appellate courts in the United States would find otherwise.

LEGAL CHALLENGES: THE SUPREME COURT VICTORY

The primary challenge to the Guantánamo detentions was brought by the Center for Constitutional Rights and was decided by the Supreme Court on June 28, 2004. The court combined the Center's case on behalf of English and Australian citizens detained in Guantánamo with a later case brought on behalf of Kuwaiti nationals.[41] Two lower courts found in favor of the government, and held that U.S. courts had no jurisdiction to hear the challenges and thus could not rule on the legality of the detentions. These courts found that U.S. courts could not hear cases brought on behalf of aliens held by the United States outside the territory of the United States. They determined that despite the U.S. government's "complete jurisdiction and control" of Guantánamo Bay, the naval base was outside the U.S. courts' authority.

These lower court rulings are quite remarkable. Despite the fact that the U.S. has imprisoned the detainees in a prison camp it totally controls, those prisoners cannot avail themselves of any court in the United States. This would leave their jailers free to hold them for any length of time and under any conditions it chooses, without recourse. There is no check on the government; it can act above the law.

The question the Supreme Court answered on June 28, 2004, is not whether the detentions are legal, but the preliminary question of whether any court in the United States can hear these cases. In a 6-3 decision, the Supreme Court found that courts in the United States have jurisdiction to consider the legality of the detentions of noncitizens detained at Guantánamo Bay Naval Base. In nonlegal language, this decision means that the detainees can argue in U.S. courts that they are being unlawfully detained.

The *New York Times*, quoting legal scholars, called the decision "the most important civil rights case in half a century." It was indeed a great victory. Until this decision, the Bush administration had argued that no court in the world could consider the legality of the Guantánamo detentions. In terms of U.S. law, it was the first time that the Supreme Court had clearly stated that noncitizens detained by the United States, outside the United States, could use the courts even during a period the administration labels "wartime."

The decision was also a major political blow to the Bush administration and its claim that it could carry on the so-called war on terror free from judicial oversight and beyond any constitutional or international constraints. It was seen in the U.S. as an important setback to the manner in which the administration is carrying out its war on terror.

The six-judge opinion was written by Justice Stevens and relied on early precedents from England. He invoked the Magna Carta, dating back to 1215, and quoted approvingly an earlier dissenting opinion, in an analogous executive detention case from 1953:

> Executive imprisonment has been considered oppressive and lawless since John, at Runnymede, pledged that no free man should be imprisoned, dispossessed, outlawed, or exiled save by the judgment of his peers or the law of the land.[42]

Despite the importance of the decision, it does not in itself spell freedom for the Guantánamo detainees; it only means that the courthouse door is now open. It is now up to the lower courts to determine whether each individual detention is lawful. We cannot predict how this will develop. The detainees' lawyers, of whom this author is one, take the position that the next proceedings ought to take place in the federal courts; that the government must come forward and justify each detention; and that each detainee has the right to an attorney and the right to contest the government's claims. To that end, on July 13, 2004, the Center for Constitutional Rights—assisted by other major law firms—filed scores of new cases on behalf of the detainees in the district court, asking for immediate access to the detainees by attorneys.

The Bush administration did not expect such an adverse ruling and initially seemed in disarray. However, on July 8, 2004, it announced plans to set up "combatant status review tribunals" at Guantánamo and began conducting these tribunals by the end of the same month. This is an obvious attempt to forestall federal court review of the cases. The tribunals are supposed to determine whether individual detainees are "enemy combatants." The hearings take place at Guantánamo before three handpicked military officers whose decision is not final, but goes to other Pentagon officials for a final ruling. Detainees do not have the right to an attorney, but instead are "assisted" by a personal representative who is a military officer and has no duty of confidentiality. The evidence used against the detainee can include hearsay, including any statements he may have made after two and a half years of detention and coercive interrogation.

This is hardly a fair system for determining whether someone should be detained indefinitely and incommunicado at Guantánamo. Without detailing all of the tribunals' deficiencies here, it seems obvious that detainees should have attorneys, that any statements made during their detention must be considered coerced and unreliable and should be suppressed, and that panels of military officers are not neutral fact-finders. In addition, the definition of "enemy combatant" for these new tribunals is meaninglessly vague, and does not comply with the recent decision of the Supreme Court in the case of Yaser Hamdi. In that case, the Court adopted a narrow definition of the term limited to those fighting against the United States in the war in Afghanistan. The Center's hope is that the detainees at Guantánamo will get a real review of their status and not the sham hearings that are now taking place. In many ways, the Guantánamo litigation is only at its beginning.

Another interesting aspect of the Supreme Court's ruling was its decision that the detainees can sue not only to test the legality of their detentions but also regarding the conditions under which they were detained. As we now know, coercive interrogation techniques, amounting to torture in some cases, were employed by the United States. The ruling in the Guantánamo cases opens the door to lawsuits by detainees to stop the use of such techniques and to try to recover money damages for their ill-treatment.

While the fight against the excesses and lawlessness of the Bush administration is far from over, the recent victory in the Supreme Court has dealt a major blow to the administration's grab for untrammeled power. The decision, while not detailing the rights a Guantánamo detainee will have, does permit writs of habeas corpus to be filed—this means the detainees will have lawyers and will have their day in court. As I write this, the lower courts are in the midst of enforcing this right. My own view, and hope, is that once civilian lawyers gain access to the detainees, it will herald the end of the interrogation camp at Guantánamo.

NOTES

1 Salim Ahmed Hamdan of Yemen, David Hicks of Australia, Ai Hamza Ahmed Sulayman al Buhlul of Yemen, and Ibrahim Ahmed Mahmoud al Qosi of Sudan have been charged with crimes ranging from conspiracy to attack civilians and murder by an unprivileged belligerent to conspiracy to commit war crimes and aiding the enemy. They are each slated to face trial by military commission, and started pretrial motions in late August 2004. The trials have been delayed by defense arguments that the judges are biased and that the trial procedures are illegal.

2 The detainees who have been charged and designated for trial by a military commission have been permitted visits by attorneys. Eleven others have been designated for commissions but not yet charged. It is assumed that these others will also see attorneys as the charging process against them goes forward. Since the Supreme Court decision in June 2004, two attorneys have been permitted access to clients not facing imminent trial by military commission. However, the Bush administration has done this gudgingly, and litigation to permit visits for many other attorneys is continuing.

3 *The History of Guantánamo Bay*, chapter 3. Available at: http://www.nsgtmo.navy.mil/gazette/History_98-64/hischp3.htm.

4 *Haitian Ctr. Council v. McNary*, 969 F.2d 1326 (2d Cir. 1992).

5 *Haitian Refugee Ctr. v. Baker*, 953 F.2d 1498 (11th Cir. 1992).

6 *Rasul v. Bush*, no. 03-334. (June 28, 2004).

7 One news story described the prisons as "three dank and overcrowded cell blocks, with a stench of unwashed bodies and from which erupt monotonous pleas for help and mercy, that more resemble cattle sheds or ill-kept stables than a jail." "258 Afghan Taliban Soldiers Released," *Reuters*, March 23, 2002. Available at http://www.dawn.com/2002/03/24/top11.htm.

8 Carlotta Gall, "A Nation Challenged: The Missing; Families Try to Trace Thousands of Missing Taliban, Many Forced to Fight," *New York Times*, February 21, 2002, A14.

9 Dana Priest and Barton Gellman, "U.S. Decries Abuse But Defends Interrogations; 'Stress and Duress' Tactics Used on Terrorism Suspects Held in Secret Overseas Facilities," *Washington Post*, December 26, 2002, A1. News reports in 2004 confirm and add much additional material on the use of torture in Bagram and other overseas U.S. detention facilities.

10 Initially most of the Guantánamo detainees were captured in Afghanistan, but by late 2002 the Department of Defense was unwilling to say from where additional captives were captured, as the following dialogue demonstrates:
      Q: "Did they come from Afghanistan?"
      Victoria Clarke, Defense Department spokesperson: "Not saying."

11 Viola Gienger, "Lawyers Contest Algerians' Handover," *Chicago Tribune*, April 11, 2002, 4.

12 Brown and Root Services, a division of the oil services company Halliburton, which was formerly headed by Vice President Cheney, is constructing the new prison. The contract may amount to $300 million. Charles Aldinger, "Halliburton to Build Cells at Guantánamo Base," Reuters, July 27, 2002.

13 Katherine Q. Seelye, "A Nation Challenged: The Prisoners; U.S. May Move Some Detainees to Domestic Military Bases," *New York Times*, January 4, 2002, A15.

14 George Edmonson, "'Gitmo' Gets a Makeover As POW Camp," Cox Washington Bureau, January 8, 2002. Available at http://www.coxnews.com/washingtonbureau/staff/edmonson/010802TER-GUANTÁNAMO.html.

15 "Rumsfeld: Afghan Detainees at Gitmo Bay Will Not Be Granted POW Status," Fox News, January 28, 2002. Available at http://www.foxnews.com/story/0,2933,44084,00.html.

16 Adam Liptak, "In First Rulings, Military Tribunals Uphold Detentions of 4," *New York Times*, August 14, 2004, A11.

17 Ibid.

18 "Return from Guantánamo Bay," June 6, 2002. Available at: http://news.bbc.co.uk/1/hi/programmes/mewsnight/2968458.stm

19 Sayed Abassin, former Guantánamo detainee, July 25, 2003. Available at: http://www.cageprisoners.com/pr_articles.php?aid=217

20 "Camp Delta: Guantánamo Bay," *60 Minutes II* September 16, 2003. Available at: www.cbsnews.com/2003/09/16/60II.

21 Greg Miller, "Many Held at Guantánamo Not likely Terrorists," *LA Times*, December 22, 2002.

22 Ibid.

23 Ibid.

24 David Rhode, "Afghans Freed from Guantánamo Speak of Heat and Isolation," *New York Times*, October 29, 2002, A18.

25 Ibid.

26 Article 71 of the Third Geneva Convention states that POWs are permitted to send not more than two letters and four cards monthly; Article 72 of that Convention also allows them to receive individual and collective relief packages containing foodstuffs, clothing, articles of a religious nature, and other similar items.

27 *See* http://www.ccr-ny.org/v2/reports/report.asp?ObjID=4bUT8M23lk&Content=424

28 "U.S.: Despite Releases, Children Still Held at Guantánamo," Human Rights Watch press release, January 29, 2004.

29 Michael Ratner, "How We Closed the Guantánamo HIV Camp: The Intersection of Politics and Litigation," *Harvard Human Rights Journal* 11, spring 1998.

30 Rhuhel Ahmed, Asif Iqbal, and Shafiq Rasul of Tipton, UK. *See* http://www.ccr-ny.org/v2/reports/report.asp?ObjID=4bUT8M23lk&Content=424.

31 Megan Lane, "Letters Home from Guantánamo Bay," BBC News Online. Available at: http://news.bbc.co.uk/1/hi/magazine/3072529.stm

32 Neil A. Lewis, "Red Cross Criticizes Indefinite Detention in Guantánamo Bay," *New York Times*, October 10, 2003.

33 Jim Teeple, "Guantánamo/Red Cross." Available at: http://www.globalsecurity.org/security/library/news/2003/10/sec-031010-3fe63cfb.htm.

34 On February 8, 2002, the day after announcement of the U.S. position, Darcy Christen, a spokesperson for the ICRC, said of the detainees: "They were captured in combat [and] we consider them prisoners of war." Richard Waddington, "Guantánamo Inmates Are POWs Despite Bush View—ICRC," Reuters, February 9, 2002.

35   The Alberto Gonzales Memo to the President, "Decision re Application of the Geneva Convention on Prisoners of War to the Conflict with al Qaeda and the Taliban," January 25 2002. Available at: http://msnbc.msn.com/id/4999148/site/newsweek/

36   *See, e.g.*, Richard Sisk, "Airport Gun Battle Firefight Erupts as Prisoners Are Flown to Cuba," *New York Daily News*, January 11, 2002, 27.

37   Katherine Q. Seelye, "Rumsfeld Backs Plan to Hold Captives Even If Acquitted," *New York Times*, March 29, 2002, A18.

38   Ibid.

39   Decision of the Inter-American Commission on Human Rights of the Organization of American States, *Detainees in Guantánamo Bay, Cuba*, March 13, 2002.

40   The Queen on the application of *Abbasi & Anor. v. Secretary of State for Foreign and Commonwealth Affairs*, [2002] EWCA Civ. 1598.

41   The law firm, Sheaman & Sterling, represented the 12 Kuwaiti nationals. Two cases were filed in federal court in Washington, D.C., and consolidated for the arguments and the decisions: *Rasul v. Bush* and *Al Odah v. United States*, 215 F.Supp. 2d 55 (D.D.C. 2002), aff'd, 321 F.3d 1134 (D.C. Cir. 2003), reversed and remanded, 124 S. Ct. 2686 (June 28, 2004).

42   Justice Stevens for the court in *Rasul v. Bush* 124 S. Ct. 2686 (June 28, 2004) quoting Justice Jackson's dissent in *Shaughnessy*

3

Statement

Maher Arar

Maher Arar is a Canadian citizen of Syrian descent who was detained by the U.S. government while transiting through JFK Airport, en route from Tunisia back home to Canada. He was arrested and interrogated by FBI and INS officers, and then deported to Syria, where he was jailed, tortured, and interrogated for months. After Syria cleared him of all connections to terrorism, he was released into Canadian custody. He is now free and back with his family.

The following statement was read by Maher Arar in Ottawa on November 4, 2003, less than one month after being released from prison in Syria.

I AM HERE TODAY to tell the people of Canada what has happened to me.

There have been many allegations made about me in the media, all of them by people who refuse to be named or come forward. So before I tell you who I am and what happened to me, I will tell you who I am not.

I am not a terrorist. I am not a member of al Qaeda and I do not know anyone who belongs to this group. All I know about al Qaeda is what I have seen in the media. I have never been to Afghanistan. I have never been anywhere near Afghanistan and I do not have any desire to ever go to Afghanistan.

Now, let me tell you who I am.

I am a Syrian-born Canadian. I moved here with my parents when I was 17 years old. I went to university and studied hard, and eventually obtained a master's degree in telecommunications. I met my wife, Monia, at McGill University. We fell in love and eventually married in 1994. I knew then that she was special, but I had no idea how special she would turn out to be.

If it were not for her I believe I would still be in prison.

We had our first child, a daughter named Barâa, in February 1997. She is six years old now. In December 1997, we moved to Ottawa from Montreal. I took a job with a high-tech firm, called the MathWorks, in Boston in 1999, and my job involved a lot of travel within the U.S.

Then in 2001 I decided to come back to Ottawa to start my own consulting company. We had our second child, Houd, in February 2002. He is 20 months old now.

So this is who I am. I am a father and a husband. I am a telecommunications engineer and entrepreneur. I have never had trouble with the police, and have always been a good citizen. So I still cannot believe what has happened to me, and how my life and career have been destroyed.

In September 2002, I was with my wife and children, and her family, vacationing in Tunisia. I got an e-mail from the MathWorks saying that they might need me soon to assess potential consulting work for one of their customers. I said good-bye to my wife and family, and headed back home to prepare for work.

I was using my air miles to travel, and the best flight I could get went from Tunisia, to Zurich, to New York, to Montreal. My flight arrived in New York at 2:00 pm on September 26, 2002. I had a few hours to wait until my connecting flight to Montreal.

This is when my nightmare began. I was pulled aside at immigration and taken to another area. Two hours later some officials came and told me this was regular procedure. They took my fingerprints and photographs.

Then some police came and searched my bags and copied my Canadian passport. I was getting worried, and I asked what was going on, and they would not answer. I asked to make a phone call, and they would not let me.

Then a team of people came and told me they wanted to ask me some questions. One man was from the FBI, and another was from the New York Police Department. I was scared and did not know what was going on. I told them I wanted a lawyer. They told me I had no right to a lawyer, because I was not an American citizen.

They asked me where I worked and how much money I made. They swore at me, and insulted me. It was very humiliating. They wanted me to answer every question quickly. They were consulting a report while they were questioning me, and the information they had was so private I thought this must be from Canada.

I told them everything I knew. They asked me about my travel in the United States. I told them about my work permits, and my business there. They asked about information on my computer and whether I was willing to share it. I welcomed the idea, but I don't know if they did.

They asked me about different people, some I know, and most I do not. They asked me about Abdullah Almalki, and I told them I worked with his brother at high-tech firms in Ottawa, and that the Almalki family had come from Syria about the same time as mine. I told them I did not know Abdullah well, but had seen him a few times and I described the times I could remember. I told them I had a casual relationship with him.

They were so rude with me, yelling at me that I had a selective memory. Then they pulled out a copy of my rental lease from 1997. I could not believe they had this. I was completely shocked. They pointed out that Abdullah had signed the lease as a witness. I had completely forgotten that he had signed it for me when we moved to Ottawa in 1997, we needed someone to witness our lease, and I phoned Abdullah's brother, and he could not come, so he sent Abdullah.

But they thought I was hiding this. I told them the truth. I had nothing to hide. I had never had problems in the United States before, and I could not believe what was happening to me. This interrogation continued until midnight. I was very, very worried, and asked for a lawyer again and again. They just ignored me. Then they put me in chains, on my wrists and ankles, and took me in a van to a place where many people were being held in another building by the airport. They would not tell me what was happening. At one o'clock in the morning they put me in a room with metal benches in it. I could not sleep. I was very, very scared and disoriented. The next morning they started questioning me again. They asked me about what I think about bin Laden, Palestine, Iraq. They also asked me about the mosques I pray in, my bank accounts, my e-mail addresses, my relatives, about everything.

This continued on and off for eight hours. Then a man from the INS came in and told me they wanted me to volunteer to go to Syria. I said no way. I said I wanted to go home to Canada or sent back to Switzerland. He said to me, "You are a special interest." They asked me to sign a form. They would not let me read it, but I just signed it. I was exhausted and confused and disoriented. I had not slept or eaten since I was in the plane. At about six in the evening they brought me some cold McDonald's meal to eat. This was the first food I had eaten since the last meal I had on the plane.

At about eight o'clock they put all the shackles and chains back on, and put me in a van, and drove me to a prison. I later learned this was the Metropolitan Detention Center. They would not tell me what was happening, or where I was going. They strip-searched me. It was humiliating. They put me in an orange suit, and took me to a doctor, where they made me sign forms, and gave me a vaccination. I asked what it was, and they would not tell me. My arm was red for almost two weeks from that.

They took me to a cell. I had never seen a prison before in my life, and I was terrified. I asked again for a phone call, and a lawyer. They just ignored me. They treated me differently than the other prisoners. They would not give me a toothbrush or toothpaste, or reading material. I did get a copy of the Qur'an about two days later.

After five days, they let me make a phone call. I called Monia's mother, who was here in Ottawa, and told her I was scared they might send me to Syria, and asked her to help find me a lawyer. They would only let me talk for two minutes.

On the seventh or eighth day they brought me a document, saying they had decided to deport me, and I had a choice of where to be deported. I wrote that I wanted to go to Canada. It asked if I had concerns about going to Canada. I wrote no, and signed it. The Canadian consul came on October 4, and I told her I was scared of being deported to Syria. She told me that would not happen. She told me that a lawyer was being arranged. I was very upset, and scared. I could barely talk.

The next day, a lawyer came. She told me not to sign any document unless she was present. We could only talk for 30 minutes. She said she would try to help me. That was a Saturday. On Sunday night at about 9:00 pm, the guards came to my cell and told me my lawyer was there to see me. I thought it was a strange time, and they took me into a room with seven or eight people in it. I asked where my lawyer was. They told me he had refused to come and started questioning me again. They said they wanted to know why I did not want to go back to Syria. I told them I would be tortured there. I told them I had not done my military service; I am a Sunni Muslim; my mother's cousin had been accused of being a member of the Muslim Brotherhood and was put in prison for nine years.

They asked me to sign a document and I refused. I told them they could not send me to Syria or I would be tortured. I asked again for a lawyer. At three in the morning they took me back to my cell. At three o'clock in the morning on Tuesday, October 8, a prison guard woke me up and told me I was leaving. They took me to another room and stripped and searched me again. Then they again chained and shackled me. Then two officials took me inside a room and read me what they said was a decision by the INS director.

They told me that based on classified information that they could not reveal to me, I would be deported to Syria. I said again that I would be tortured there. Then they read part of the document where it explained that INS was not the body that deals with Geneva Conventions regarding torture.

Then they took me outside into a car and drove me to an airport in New Jersey. Then they put me on a small private jet. I was the only person on the plane with them. I was still chained and shackled. We flew first to Washington. A new team of people got on the plane and the others left. I overheard them talking on the phone, saying that Syria was refusing to take me directly, but Jordan would take me.

Then we flew to Portland, to Rome, and then to Amman, Jordan. All the time I was on the plane I was thinking how to avoid being tortured. I was very scared. We landed in Amman at three o'clock in the morning local time on October 9.

They took me out of the plane and there were six or seven Jordanian men waiting for us. They blindfolded and chained me, and put me in a van. They made me bend my head down in the backseat. Then, these men started beating me. Every time I tried to talk they beat me. For the first few minutes it was very intense.

Thirty minutes later we arrived at a building where they took off my blindfold and asked routine questions, before taking me to a cell. It was around four-thirty in the morning on October 9. Later that day, they took my fingerprints, and blindfolded me and put me in a van. I asked where I was going, and they told me I was going back to Montreal.

About 45 minutes later, I was put into a different car. These men started beating me again. They made me keep my head down, and it was very uncomfortable, but every time I moved, they beat me again. Over an hour later we arrived at what I think was the border with Syria. I was put in another car and we drove for another three hours. I was taken into a building, where some guards went through my bags and took some chocolates I bought in Zurich.

I asked one of the people where I was and he told me I was in the Palestine branch of the Syrian military intelligence. It was now about six o'clock in the evening on October 9. Three men came and took me into a room. I was very, very scared. They put me on a chair, and one of the men started asking me questions. I later learned this man was a colonel. He asked me about my brothers, and why we had left Syria. I answered all the questions.

If I did not answer quickly enough, he would point to a metal chair in the corner and ask, "Do you want me to use this?" I did not know then what that chair was for. I learned later it was used to torture people. I asked him what he wanted to hear. I was terrified, and I did not want to be tortured. I would say anything to avoid torture. This lasted for four hours. There was no violence, only threats this day. At about 1 o'clock in the morning, the guards came to take me to my cell downstairs.

We went into the basement, and they opened a door, and I looked in. I could not believe what I saw. I asked how long I would be kept in this place. He did not answer, but put me in and closed the door. It was like a grave. It had no light. It was three feet wide. It was six feet deep.

It was seven feet high. It had a metal door, with a small opening in the door, which did not let in light because there was a piece of metal on the outside for sliding things into the cell.

There was a small opening in the ceiling, about one foot by two feet with iron bars. Over that was another ceiling, so only a little light came through this. There were cats and rats up there, and from time to time the cats peed through the opening into the cell. There were two blankets, two dishes, and two bottles. One bottle was for water and the other one was used for urinating during the night. Nothing else. No light.

I spent 10 months and 10 days inside that grave.

The next day I was taken upstairs again. The beating started that day and was very intense for a week, and then less intense for another week. That second and the third days were the worst. I could hear other prisoners being tortured, and screaming and screaming.

Interrogations are carried out in different rooms. One tactic they use is to question prisoners for two hours, and then put them in a waiting room, so they can hear the others screaming, and then bring them back to continue the interrogation.

The cable is a black electrical cable, about two inches thick. They hit me with it everywhere on my body. They mostly aimed for my palms, but sometimes missed and hit my wrists. They were sore and red for three weeks. They also struck me on my hips, and lower back. Interrogators constantly threatened me with the metal chair, tire, and electric shocks.

The tire is used to restrain prisoners while they torture them with beating on the sole of their feet. I guess I was lucky, because they put me in the tire, but only as a threat. I was not beaten while in the tire. They used the cable on the second and third day, and after that mostly beat me with their hands, hitting me in the stomach and on the back of my neck, and slapping me on the face. Where they hit me with the cables, my skin turned blue for two or three weeks, but there was no bleeding. At the end of the day they told me tomorrow would be worse. So I could not sleep.

Then on the third day, the interrogation lasted about 18 hours. They beat me from time to time and make me wait in the waiting room for one to two hours before resuming the interrogation. While in the waiting room I heard a lot of people screaming. They wanted me to say I went to Afghanistan. This was a surprise to me. They had not asked about this in the United States.

They kept beating me so I had to falsely confess and told them I did go to Afghanistan. I was ready to confess to anything if it would stop the torture. They wanted me to say I went to a training camp. I was so scared I urinated on myself twice. The beating was less severe each of the following days.

At the end of each day, they would always say, "Tomorrow will be harder for you." So each night, I could not sleep. I did not sleep for the first four days, and slept no more than two hours a day for about two months. Most of time I was not taken back to my cell, but to the waiting room where I could hear all the prisoners being tortured and screaming.

One time, I heard them banging a man's head repeatedly on a desk really hard. Around October 17, the beatings subsided. Their next tactic was to take me in a room, blindfolded, and people would talk about me. I could hear them saying, "He knows lots of people who are terrorists; we will get their numbers; he is a liar; he has been out of the country for long."

Then they would say, "Let's be frank, let's be friends, tell us the truth," and come around the desk, and slap me on the face. They played lots of mind games. The interrogation and beating ended three days before I had my first consular visit, on October 23.

I was taken from my cell and my beard was shaved. I was taken to another building, and there was the colonel in the hallway with some other men and they all seemed very nervous and agitated.

I did not know what was happening and they would not tell me. They never say what is happening. You never know what will happen next. I was told not to tell anything about the beating, then I was taken into a room for a ten-minute meeting with the consul. The colonel was there, and three other Syrian officials including an interpreter. I cried a lot at that meeting. I could not say anything about the torture. I thought if I did, I would not get any more visits, or I might be beaten again.

After that visit, about a month after I arrived, they called me up to sign and place my thumbprint on a document about seven pages long. They would not let me read it, but I had to put my thumbprint and signature on the bottom of each page. It was handwritten.

Another document was about three pages long, with questions: Who are your friends? How long have you been out of the country? Last question was empty lines. They answered the questions with their own handwriting except for the last one where I was forced to write that I had been to Afghanistan.

The consular visits were my lifeline, but I also found them very frustrating. There were seven consular visits, and one visit from members of Parliament. After the visits I would bang my head and my fist on the wall in frustration. I needed the visits, but I could not say anything there.

I got new clothes after the December 10 consular visit. Until then, I had been wearing the same clothes since being on the jet from the United States.

On three different occasions in December I had a very hard time. Memories crowded my mind and I thought I was going to lose control, and I just screamed and screamed. I could not breathe well after, and felt very dizzy.

I was not exposed to sunlight for six months. The only times I left the grave was for interrogation, and for the visits. Daily life in that place was hell. When I was detained in New York I weighed about 180 pounds. I think I lost about 40 pounds while I was at the Palestine Branch.

On August 19 I was taken upstairs to see the investigator, and I was given a paper and asked to write what he dictated. If I protested, he kicked me. I was forced to write that I went to a training camp in Afghanistan. They made me sign and put my thumbprint on the last page.

The same day I was transferred to a different place, which I learnt later was the Investigation Branch. I was placed there in a 12 feet by 20 feet collective cell. We were about 50 people in that place. The next day I was taken to the Sednaya prison. I was very lucky that I was not tortured when I arrived there. All the other prisoners were tortured when they arrived.

Sednaya prison was like heaven for me. I could move around, and talk with other prisoners. I could buy food to eat and I gained a lot of weight there. I was only beaten once there.

On around September 19 or 20, I heard the other prisoners saying that another Canadian had arrived there. I looked up, and saw a man, but I did not recognize him. His head was shaved, and he was very, very thin and pale. He was very weak. When I looked closer, I recognized him. It was Abdullah Almalki. He told me he had also been at the Palestine Branch, and that he had also been in a grave like I had been except he had been in it longer.

He told me he had been severely tortured with the tire, and the cable. He was also hanged upside down. He was tortured much worse than me. He had also been tortured when he was brought to Sednaya, so that was only two weeks before.

I do not know why they have Abdullah there. What I can say for sure is that no human deserves to be treated the way he was, and I hope that Canada does all they can to help him.

On September 28 I was taken out and blindfolded and put in what felt like a bus and taken back to the Palestine Branch. They would not tell me what was happening, and I was scared I was going back to the grave. Instead, I was put in one of the waiting rooms where they torture people. I could hear the prisoners being tortured, and screaming, again.

The same day I was called into an office to answer more questions, about what I would say if I came back to Canada. They did not tell me I would be released.

I was put back in the waiting room, and I was kept there for one week, listening to all the prisoners screaming. It was awful.

On Sunday, October 5 I was taken out and into a car and driven to a court. I was put in a room with a prosecutor. I asked for a lawyer and he said I did not need one. I asked what was going on and he read from my confession. I tried to argue I was beaten and did not go to Afghanistan, but he did not listen. He did not tell me what I was charged with, but told me to stamp my fingerprint and sign on a document he would not let me see.

Then he said I would be released.

Then I was taken back to the Palestine Branch where I met the head of the Syrian Military Intelligence and officials from the Canadian embassy. And then I was released. I want to conclude by thanking all of the people who worked for my release, especially my wife, Monia, and human rights groups, and all the people who wrote letters, and all the members of Parliament who stood up for justice.

Of course I thank all of the journalists for covering my story.

The past year has been a nightmare, and I have spent the past few weeks at home trying to learn how to live with what happened to me. I know that the only way I will ever be able to move on in my life and have a future is if I can find out why this happened to me.

I want to know why this happened to me. I believe the only way I can ever know why this happened is to have all the truth come out in a public inquiry.

My priority right now is to clear my name, get to the bottom of the case, and make sure this does not happen to any other Canadian citizens in the future. I believe the best way to go about achieving this goal is to put pressure on the government to call for a public inquiry.

What is at stake here is the future of our country, the interests of Canadian citizens, and most importantly Canada's international reputation for being a leader in human rights where citizens from different ethnic groups are treated no different than other Canadians.

Thank you for your patience.

4

Torture, "Stress and Duress," and Rendition as Counter-Terrorism Tools

Steven Macpherson Watt

"All told, more than three thousand suspected terrorists have been arrested in many countries. Many others have met a different fate. Let's put it this way—they are no longer a problem to the United States and our friends and allies. . . . We have the terrorists on the run. We're keeping them on the run. One by one, the terrorists are learning the meaning of American justice."

—President George W. Bush, State of the Union Address, January 28, 2003

"The United States is committed to the worldwide elimination of torture and we are leading this fight by example. I call on all governments to join with the United States and the community of law-abiding nations in prohibiting, investigating, and prosecuting all acts of torture and in undertaking to prevent other cruel and unusual punishment."

—President George W. Bush, United Nations International Day in Support of Victims of Torture, June 26, 2003

INTRODUCTION

Since the U.S. attack and invasion of Afghanistan in October 2001, the U.S. military, together with the FBI and the CIA, has arrested and detained persons whom it suspects of being either members of al Qaeda or the Taliban armed forces.[1] The objective of these measures has been to interrogate detainees to secure information on the al Qaeda network and prevent possible future terrorist attacks.[2] All three government agencies are actively involved in the interrogation process,[3] as are private corporations, such as Titan Corporation and CACI, contracted by the Department of Defense.[4]

Thousands of individuals suspected of being members of al Qaeda or their supporters have been detained worldwide since the attacks of September 11, 2001.[5] These suspects are detained at U.S. government detention facilities at Bagram Air Force Base in Afghanistan, Guantánamo Bay Naval Base in Cuba, and Diego Garcia, an Indian Ocean isle, and other undisclosed secret facilities around the world.[6] Around 550 of these suspects we know are incarcerated at Guantánamo Bay, Cuba. The numbers held elsewhere are not known.

To date, none of the suspects have been brought before a court, military or otherwise.[7] They simply languish in legal limbo. As discussed in chapter 2, the U.S. government has refused to recognize any of them as prisoners of war (POWs), or to extend to them the protections of the Geneva Conventions. None have been charged with a crime or afforded the opportunity to challenge the legality of their detention. The government's official position is that they are all "enemy combatants" who may be held until the conclusion of the "war on terrorism." During this time the government states that they will be treated humanely and in a manner consistent with the principles of the Third Geneva Convention.[8] As described in earlier chapters, the day-to-day reality of their detention is something entirely different.

THE USE OF TORTURE AND OTHER CRUEL, INHUMAN, OR DEGRADING TREATMENT BY THE UNITED STATES SINCE SEPTEMBER 11

For nongovernmental organizations involved in monitoring the post-9/11 actions of the United States, the Iraq prison abuses are the horrific culmination of a long history of mistreatment of detainees in U.S. custody. Since early 2002, media reports have documented a pattern of abuse by United States forces in Afghanistan almost identical to the abuses committed by the U.S. at the Abu Ghraib prison.[9] For example, in late 2002, an in-depth article in the *Washington Post* revealed that persons detained and interrogated at the U.S. military base at Bagram had been subjected to treatment amounting to torture or at the very least, cruel, inhuman, or degrading treatment or punishment.[10] U.S. officials told reporters that during interrogations they routinely resort to the use of violence and consider such an approach to be "just and necessary." One official interviewed is quoted as saying, "If you don't violate someone's human rights some of the time, you probably aren't doing your job."[11]

U.S. officials interviewed said that persons interrogated were routinely subjected to what they termed "stress and duress" techniques, including "standing or kneeling for hours" while wearing black hoods or opaque goggles, being "held in awkward, painful positions," and being deprived of sleep with loud noises or a 24-hour bombardment of lights. The report states that prior to their incarceration and interrogation, captives were often "softened up" by members of the Military Police and U.S. Army Special Forces troops, by being beaten and confined in tiny rooms. U.S. military personnel have also blindfolded and thrown detainees into walls.[12]

THE BUSH ADMINISTRATION'S RESPONSE TO ALLEGATIONS OF THE USE OF TORTURE

The *Washington Post* article was not a two-paragraph puff piece, but rather an in-depth exposé compiled as a result of the reporters' visit to Afghanistan and their interviews with at least ten current U.S. national security officials, as well as several former intelligence officials. The CIA, which continues to have primary responsibility for interrogations of detainees in Afghanistan and elsewhere, declined to comment for the piece. U.S. officials, when asked for comment, without elaborating on specifics simply stated that it contained "many inaccuracies."[13]

At the time, neither President Bush nor any other high-ranking official in the U.S. administration saw fit to respond to the specific allegations made, nor did they challenge the report's veracity. Prompted by the article, Human Rights Watch wrote to the president on December 26, 2002, asking that he clarify, among other things, U.S. policy vis-à-vis torture and commit to carrying out an investigation and holding accountable persons found responsible for torture.[14] In his April 2, 2003, response on behalf of the president, William J. Haynes II, general counsel to the Department of Defense, wrote, "United States policy condemns and prohibits torture" and that "[w]hen questioning enemy combatants, U.S. personnel are required to follow this policy and applicable laws prohibiting torture." Interestingly, while Mr. Hayes addressed the issue of U.S. policy on the use of torture, he said nothing about its position on the mistreatment of detainees that falls short of torture, such as the use of so-called stress and duress techniques.[15] In not categorically denouncing all forms of mistreatment of detainees, Mr. Hayes suggests that the United States permits cruel, inhuman, or degrading treatment. Moreover, in the light of the Abu Ghraib scandal—even in regard to torture—Mr. Hayes's reassurances now ring hollow.

In March 2002, Secretary of Defense Donald Rumsfeld dismissed claims of detainee abuse at Guantánamo as "based on the shrill hyperventilation of a few people who didn't know what they were talking about."[16] Even when concerns were voiced by a senior member of the military in the fall of 2002, they were given short shrift. In October 2002, the commander of Camp Delta at Guantánamo Bay, Brigadier General Rick Baccus, was removed from duty allegedly due to his concerns about detainee mistreatment by their interrogators.[17] The administration's response was not to conduct an investigation into the allegations, but simply to state that Major Baccus was removed because he was surplus to requirements.

Even the graphic pictures of U.S. soldiers abusing detainees are not unique to Iraq. As far back as 2002, photographs of John Walker Lindh, the so-called American Taliban, naked, blindfolded, bound, and tied to a stretcher were plastered across national newspapers.[18] "Traitor" and "Rat" screamed one headline in the *New York Post*. Inside, the tabloid's star columnist urged authorities to "put him before a military tribunal, get him up against the wall and drill him like a sieve."[19]

During Lindh's trial his lawyers described how, after capturing him, U.S. forces "blindfolded and bound [him] with plastic cuffs so tight they cut off the circulation to his hands." They also stated that he was threatened with death and torture and that when he was held at the U.S. base he was "blindfolded and restrained in a metal shipping container without heat or light, immobilized by shackles and bound naked to a stretcher" for two or three days. No one seemed to care about Lindh's mistreatment, nor were those responsible ever reprimanded or disciplined. During the plea bargain which landed Lindh a twenty-year sentence, the prosecution's primary concern was that none of the descriptions of his abuse leak out into the public domain. In terms of his plea agreement, Lindh "puts to rest his claims of mistreatment by the United States military, and all claims of mistreatment are withdrawn."[20]

The reason behind the United States' failure to take seriously and fully investigate the many credible allegations about the torture of detainees came dramatically to light early in 2004. A series of legal memoranda authored by lawyers at the Pentagon and Department of Justice set forth a framework that, quite incredibly, officially sanctioned the use of interrogation techniques that amount to torture or inhumane treatment.

Two of the earliest of these legal memoranda, dated January 22, 2002 and February 7, 2002, analyzed the application of treaties and laws to al Qaeda and Taliban detainees and specifically addressed the issue of the legal status of individuals detained in the "war on terrorism." In essence, these memos set forth a framework for holding prisoners outside the protections of the rule of law and gave the go-ahead for the torture and ill-treatment of persons detained in connection with the "war on terrorism." They established the platform for the horrific abuses perpetrated against prisoners in Afghanistan, Guantánamo Bay, and finally Abu Ghraib. In them, Assistant Attorney General Jay S. Bybee stated that President Bush has "the authority under the Constitution" to "suspend" the Geneva Conventions in the conflict with Afghanistan. Thus these memoranda claim that President Bush as commander in chief has the power to simply and unilaterally cast aside centuries-old rules devised to ensure that even in the midst of the horrors of war, certain fundamental elements of humanity remain intact. They sanction the position that certain detainees may not legally be entitled to humane treatment, and United States officers need only treat them humanely when consistent with military necessity.[21]

Several months later, Bybee, who was later appointed by President Bush as a federal judge in the 9th Circuit Court of Appeals in Las Vegas, authored an even more shocking memorandum. In this memorandum, dated August 1, 2002, Bybee reasoned that inflicting moderate or fleeting pain does not constitute torture. Under a federal law that criminalizes torture, the Torture Act,

Bybee claimed that an act "must be equivalent in intensity to the pain accompanying serious physical injury, such as organ failure, impairment of bodily function or even death," before falling within the act's definition of torture. Not only does such a narrow definition redefine U.S. law, it flies in the face of accepted notions of what constitutes torture under international law. Bybee also argued that torture is unlawful only if the infliction of pain is the offender's specific objective: "[e]ven if the defendant knows that severe pain will result from his actions, if causing such harm is not his objective, he lacks the requisite specific intent." Finally, the memorandum discusses ways by which government officials could escape criminal and civil liability for acts of torture by relying on potential defenses, including necessity and self-defense. At the end of the day, Bybee asserts that the President, pursuant to his powers as commander in chief, has carte blanche to order torture notwithstanding treaties and laws barring it.[22]

From this point onward a slew of similar memoranda emanated from the Pentagon and the Department of Justice describing a number of interrogation techniques that the United States considered "legally available." Perhaps the most detailed of these was a Defense Department memorandum approved by Defense Secretary Donald H. Rumsfeld dated December 2, 2002. In it, those techniques given official imprimatur included the use of stress positions; sensory deprivation; isolation for 30 days, or more upon approval; removal of clothing; hooding; "forced grooming"; "[t]he use of scenarios designed to convince the detainee that death or severely painful consequences are imminent for him and/or his family"; "[e]xposure to cold weather or water"; and "[u]se of a wet towel and dripping water to induce the misconception of suffocation."[23] All these techniques were subsequently termed euphemistically by the military as "stress and duress" techniques.

STRESS AND DURESS: WHAT IS IT?

Simply put, "stress and duress" is the post-9/11 term for officially sanctioned torture and other ill-treatment. U.S. officials were quite happy to talk openly with journalists about the treatment the term incorporates; this is quite understandable now that we know that the techniques have been "legally" vetted and sanctioned at the highest levels of government.

In March 2003, the *New York Times* interviewed the then U.S. commander of the coalition forces in Afghanistan, Lieutenant General Daniel K. McNeill,[24] about treatment of prisoners. Interviewed at Bagram Air Base, General McNeill affirmed that prisoners at Bagram had been made to stand for extended periods, sometimes in awkward positions. The article also includes interviews with two individuals who were once detained at the Bagram facility. They alleged that as many as one hundred prisoners were held at the time of their detention and that "they had been made to stand hooded, their arms raised and chained to the ceiling, their feet shackled, unable to move for hours at a time, day and night."[25] Describing in detail the inside of the facility, one of them said that he had been kept naked the entire time and that he had been kept standing for 10 days "until his legs became so swollen that the shackles around his ankles tightened and stopped the blood flow."[26] Both claimed to have been repeatedly kicked by their U.S. guards and interrogators during their interrogation as well as being kept from sleeping.

Sleep deprivation and psychological manipulation were among two interrogation techniques that U.S. officials told the *New York Times* they planned to use on the captured al Qaeda suspect, Khalid Sheikh Mohammed.[27] At the time, Mr. Mohammed was reported to be in the custody of the CIA at an undisclosed location outside Pakistan. During his interrogation, officials said that "they expected the Central Intelligence Agency to use every means at its disposal,

short of what it considers outright torture, to try and crack him."
Another U.S. official interviewed said that "[t]here are a lot of ways
short of torturing someone to get information from a subject."[28]
In a second *Times* article published just days later, senior officials
were again quoted as stating that while Mr. Mohammed's interrogators would not subject him to physical torture, they would rely on
"what they consider acceptable techniques like sleep and light deprivation and the temporary withholding of food, water, access to
sunlight and medical attention."[29]

As can be seen, for some two and a half years the domestic and
international press have reported on the mistreatment of detainees
in U.S. custody, and for two and half years the administration has done
its best to deflect, deny, or ignore the reports. The allegations are
specific in nature and identify a number of techniques that appear
to have the government's blessing. These techniques include:

- beatings
- "water boarding," in which a prisoner is strapped, forcibly
  submerged underwater, and made to believe he might
  drown[30]
- transfer to detention facilities in unventilated boxes
- preincarceration solitary confinement in small rooms
- stripping detainees naked and subjecting them to humiliation
- sensory deprivation during transfer, including blindfolding
  and hooding
- prolonged shackling of detainees' hands and feet
- forced standing or kneeling for extended periods of time
- forced holding in awkward, painful positions
- sensory deprivation techniques, including hooding and the
  wearing of blackened goggles
- sleep deprivation
- subjecting detainees to extremes of temperature
- prolonged incommunicado detention

DEATHS IN U.S. CUSTODY

More horrifying still are reports not merely of the mistreatment of detainees but of their murder while in U.S. custody. In December 2002 two detainees, a 22-year-old Afghan man and another aged about 30, died at the Bagram Air Base under suspicious circumstances—one from pulmonary embolism and the other from a heart attack. The U.S. military handed their bodies back to their families with death certificates stipulating the cause of death in each case was "homicide" and that "blunt force injuries" were present. Both the autopsies as well as the certificates were completed by a U.S. Army pathologist.[31] Criminal investigations by the military into the deaths were "still in progress" in late June 2003.[32] According to a recent *New York Times* article, these investigations are still ongoing and are being conducted by the military, together with nine other "possible homicides linked to interrogation practices in Iraq and Afghanistan."[33] In June 2004, no doubt influenced by the public outcry over the Iraq prison abuses and calls for accountability, Attorney General John Ashcroft himself announced the indictment of a contractor working for the CIA on charges stemming from the death of one detainee, Abdul Wali. The four-count indictment states that the contractor, David Passaro, beat Mr. Wali repeatedly using his hands, feet, and a large flashlight during interrogations on June 19 and June 20, 2003, at a U.S. detention facility near Asadabad in the northeastern Kunar Province, Afghanistan.[34] Passaro's trial has yet to proceed.

TORTURE BY ANOTHER NAME: "RENDITION"

As an alternative or in addition to the use of "stress and duress" techniques during interrogations, the United States has resorted to the transfer or "rendition" of detainees to the governments of

countries such as Jordan, Egypt, Morocco, and Syria—countries
the United States has long criticized for human rights abuses,
including the use of torture. The rationale behind this process was
explained by one U.S. official actually involved in the practice:
"We don't kick the [expletive] out of them. We send them to
other countries so that they can kick the [expletive] out of
them."[35] Another official also involved in the practice said that he
knew that captives who were rendered would probably be tortured:
"I . . . do it with my eyes open," he said.[36]

The countries to which detainees are rendered are not randomly selected; rather, they are carefully chosen by the U.S.
depending on the purpose of the rendition in question. Former
CIA agent Robert Baer, who worked covertly for the United
States throughout the Middle East until the mid-1990s, explained
that Jordan is the preferred destination for detainees when the
United States wants "a serious interrogation"; Syria if it wants
them tortured; and Egypt when it wants "someone to disappear—
never to see them again."[37]

The concept of "rendition" has no fixed meaning under domestic or international law. In the post-9/11 era, the Bush administration has adopted the phrase as a term of art in much the same way
as it has the term "enemy combatant." Essentially, the United States
uses the term "rendition" to describe its practice of transferring
terrorist suspects to a foreign government in order to obtain information from them by interrogation methods that are morally and
legally unacceptable in this country. In other words, rendition is a
mechanism used to outsource torture to other governments.

Under this extralegal policy, even after being "rendered" the
detainee remains under the ultimate control of the United States.
In discussing the interrogation of a terrorist suspect rendered by
the United States to Saudi Arabia, a senior U.S. official stated that
the CIA is "still very much in control" and that they will often "feed
questions to their investigators."[38]

The "rendition" of criminal suspects by the United States is not a new phenomenon. Used as an alternative to lawful extradition, the term was an invention of President Clinton's national security adviser, Sandy Berger, who described the practice as a "new art form." The first recorded rendition arrests began in Tirana, Albania, in July 1998 when a team of CIA operatives in collaboration with Albania's secret police foiled an alleged plan by five suspected Egyptian Islamic militants to blow up the U.S. embassy with a car bomb. After their capture and torture at the hands of the Albanian secret police, the CIA flew the five to Egypt and handed them over to the Egyptian government. All were subsequently tortured and summarily executed by the Egyptian authorities.[39]

Since September 11, there appears to have been a dramatic increase in resorting to this shadowy practice. The first detailed media reports on post-9/11 renditions appeared in 2002. All concerned renditions of individuals suspected of al Qaeda membership, and all took place between the United States and foreign powers outside U.S. sovereign territory. In March 2002, the *Washington Post* first reported on U.S. involvement in seizing terrorism suspects in third countries and shipping them off with little if any legal process or protections to countries—including Syria, Pakistan, and Egypt—where torture of detainees is routine.[40] In November 2002, the *New York Times* reported that Mohammed Heidar Zammar, a dual German-Syrian citizen allegedly involved in terrorist activities in Germany, was seized in Morocco and rendered to Syria at the behest of the United States.[41] In January 2003, two prominent alleged al Qaeda operatives, Abu Zubaydah and Ramzi Binalshibh, were reported to have been captured in Pakistan with the cooperation of Pakistani officials and then transferred to a U.S. detention facility at an unknown location.[42]

More recently, in his testimony before the 9/11 Commission, George Tenet, then director of the CIA, spoke openly about the practice and praised it as one of the United States' key counter-terrorism policies. In his testimony, Tenet stated that in an unspec-ified period before September 11, the United States had undertaken over 70 such renditions, adding that the CIA had "racked up many successes, including the rendition of many dozens of terrorists prior to September 11, 2001."[43]

A few specific examples serve to illustrate how the policy of ren-dition is being implemented and the impact it has on the subjects and members of their families. As will be seen, many of the vic-tims of rendition end up at Guantánamo after being arrested in countries—including South Asian, African, and European nations—far from the Afghanistan theater of war. This evidence contradicts the administration's insistence that all those detained at Guantánamo were picked up on the battlefield with guns in their hands.[44]

For example, on January 18, 2002, six Algerians, several of whom also possessed Bosnian citizenship, were handed over by Bosnian police to the NATO Stabilization Force in direct viola-tion of an order by the Human Rights Chamber for Bosnia and Herzegovina. The men were later transferred to the custody of the U.S. military, which then transported them to Guantánamo. The Human Rights Chamber had ordered that four of the men should not be removed from Bosnia pending its final decision on the case. As this case illustrates, the United States has engaged in renditions despite pending legal proceedings prohibiting this removal.

The circumstances surrounding two British residents' rendi-tion from The Gambia, Africa, are also quite extraordinary. On November 8, 2002, Bisher Al-Rawi, an Iraqi national legally res-ident in the UK, Jamil Al-Banna, a Jordanian national with refugee status in the UK, and a business associate, Abdullah El-Janoudi, a UK national, were arrested in The Gambia by members of the Gambian National Intelligence Agency (NIA) upon arriving at Banjul Airport. A fourth man, Bisher Al-Rawi's brother, Wahab

Al-Rawi, also a UK national, who had arrived in The Gambia some days earlier and who had gone to the airport to meet them, was also arrested. The four men, all of whom are resident in the UK, had traveled to The Gambia in connection with the management of a peanut processing company that Wahab Al-Rawi had established there.

After an initial period of interrogation by Gambian agents at NIA headquarters in Banjul, the interrogation was taken over by U.S. agents. The men were held in several different undisclosed locations in Banjul during this time. At least one was threatened by U.S. investigators that unless he cooperated he would be handed over to the Gambian police, who would beat and rape him. The U.S. agents also reportedly "apologized" for injuries sustained by one of the suspects during what they termed "a scuffle" with his Gambian guards.

Sometime in early December 2002, Wahab Al-Rawi and Abdullah El-Janoudi, the two British nationals, were released without charge. Both returned to the UK. According to Mr. Al-Rawi, although Gambian officials were present, the entire detention and interrogation process was controlled not by the Gambians but by U.S. agents.[45]

For about two months, Bisher Al-Rawi and Jamil Al-Banna were held incommunicado in Banjul while being interrogated by U.S. agents on their alleged links with al Qaeda. In early January 2003, Amnesty International received information indicating that both men had been secretly transferred to the U.S. military base at Bagram. U.S. officials contacted by Amnesty refused to confirm the whereabouts of the two men.

Bisher and Jamil's rendition to Bagram took place before either of them had been permitted to consult with a lawyer, before any independent review of any evidence against them, and despite the fact that a *habeas corpus* petition on their behalf was pending in the Gambian courts.[46] Sometime at the beginning of 2003, both men were transferred to Guantánamo, where they remain to this day.

On June 22, 2003, five men—two Turkish nationals, a Saudi, a Sudanese national, and a Kenyan national—were arrested in Blantyre, Malawi, by Malawi's National Intelligence Bureau and U.S. agents. The men were suspected of being members of al Qaeda. Initially held at an undisclosed location in Malawi without access to lawyers, the five were secretly transferred out of the country on June 24, 2003, first to Zimbabwe for a month and then to Sudan. They were eventually released after no evidence linking them to al Qaeda was found. These renditions took place despite an order of the High Court of Blantyre issued shortly after their arrest and requiring that they be brought before it 48 hours later.

In a letter dated June 26, 2003, in response to an inquiry by Amnesty International into the rendition, an official of the Malawian government wrote that although agents of the Malawian government were involved in the arrests it was "U.S.A. Secret Agents who controlled the whole operation," including the arrest, detention, and transfer and interrogations in Malawi and beyond. The official stated that his government was not in a position to control the operation and that the government felt compelled to cooperate with the United States as part of its contribution to the worldwide fight against terrorism.[47] Sadly, the letter suggests that the Malawian government deemed it appropriate to sacrifice even the most fundamental human rights in the name of counterterrorism.

In the implementation of its rendition policy, the United States has not restricted itself to countries such as Bosnia and Malawi, over which the United States exerts considerable influence and which have dubious human rights records. In May 2004, Swedish Television reported that in December 2001, U.S. agents and a U.S. government–leased Gulfstream V jet airplane were involved in the abduction and transportation of two Egyptian terrorism suspects from Sweden to Egypt.[48] The Swedish government, which has long prided itself on its human rights record, did nothing to prevent U.S. involvement in the unlawful removal of two individuals within its jurisdiction to Egypt, a country that Sweden knows practices torture. In Egypt the two men, both of whom had been seeking asylum in Sweden, were incarcerated in Cairo's notorious Tora prison and tortured during interrogation.[49]

The whole process was carried out outside Sweden's normal legal channels. The two men were grabbed on the streets of Stockholm at 5:00 pm and were bound for Egypt without notice to their appointed legal counsel shortly before 10:00 pm the very same day. According to classified documents recently released by the Swedish government, the United States played a central role in the whole affair, not only by providing the plane but also through the provision of personnel and logistical support. The plane itself was registered to a Massachusetts company, Premier Executive Transport Services, a firm with two registered aircraft and permission to land them at any U.S. military base around the world. Swedish Television revealed that two months earlier the very same plane had been used to transport a Yemeni suspect from Pakistan to Jordan.[50]

Some two years after the events, the now-embarrassed Swedish government is calling for an international inquiry into the incident, possibly under the auspices of the United Nations. The Swedish Parliament has also convened an internal investigation into the role played by U.S. intelligence agents. U.S. officials, on the other hand, have remained silent, declining to comment even in the face of Swedish government documentation confirming U.S. participation.[51]

In Europe, Africa, and Pakistan, court proceedings have also failed to prevent the United States from carrying out its rendition policy. In early 2002, Moazzam Begg, a 35-year-old man holding dual UK-Pakistan citizenship, was seized from his apartment in

Islamabad, Pakistan, by Pakistani and U.S. agents. Moazzam had traveled to Pakistan with his family in early 2001 to establish a school for disadvantaged children and to assist in the Afghan refugee crisis. Moazzam was arrested in the middle of the night in front of his wife, Sally, and their two young children. He was bundled into the trunk of a car and driven away to an undisclosed location. Shortly thereafter a habeas corpus petition was filed on his behalf with the courts in Pakistan, challenging the legality of his detention and demanding that his captors immediately account for his whereabouts. Despite this pending legal proceeding, in early February 2002, Moazzam was transferred out of Pakistan and into U.S. custody at its air force base in Kandahar, Afghanistan. On February 6, 2003, Moazzam was moved again to the U.S. military base at Bagram, Afghanistan. While in custody, Moazzam's mental health deteriorated significantly. He was detained for a year without access to a lawyer, his family, or any court.[52] He wrote that he was feeling increasingly depressed and hopeless and that he had been subjected to bright artificial lights for extended periods of time.[53] Most of what Moazzam wrote was subject to heavy censorship, so his family was unable to get a clear picture of the true horror of his incarceration.

On February 11, 2003, Moazzam's father, a retired bank manager from Birmingham, England, received a short message on his answering machine from the UK Foreign Office; his son had been transferred to Camp Delta, Guantánamo on February 6, 2003. In July 2003, Moazzam was designated for trial before a military commission. Since this time no charges have been laid against him, he simply languishes indefinitely in his island prison.[54]

More worryingly still have been accounts of the United States rendering people to countries with the express purpose that they be interrogated under torture. Interviews with former Guantánamo detainees, Shafiq Rasul and Asif Iqbal, who were returned to England from Guantánamo, in March 2004, and whose testimonies appear earlier in this book, shed light on the details surrounding Australian citizen Mamdouh Habib's rendition to Guantánamo from Pakistan in 2002.

A fifty-four-year-old former Egyptian citizen, Mamdouh traveled to Pakistan in early August 2001 from his home in Sydney, Australia, to look for schools for his teenage children. Alarmed by the possibility of the imminent outbreak of armed conflict in the region, Mamdouh called his wife, Maha, to say that he was returning early and would be catching a flight back home on October 4, 2001. This was the last time she heard his voice.

From information relayed to her by the Australian government, Maha learned that Pakistani police had arrested Mamdouh in Pakistan. They did not explain why, however. Maha was told that Mamdouh was transferred from Pakistan to Egypt, from there to Bagram in Afghanistan, and eventually, in May 2002, to Guantánamo.[55] However, in conversations among Mamdouh and Shafiq and Asif, Mamdouh revealed that U.S. agents had flown him to Egypt, where he was subjected to interrogation under torture before being handed back to the Americans and flown to Guantánamo. The last his wife and family heard from Mamdouh was a short note from Guantánamo in May 2003.[56]

For the most part, the Bush administration has confined the exercise of its rendition policy to terrorist suspects located outside U.S. territory. Recently, however, it has shown no respect for such bounds.

In October 2002, in the face of strong diplomatic protests by the Canadian government, the United States removed Maher Arar, a Canadian citizen of Syrian descent, to Syria.[57] As his testimony in chapter 3 describes, Maher was arrested, detained, and interrogated by officials from U.S. Immigration and the FBI before being placed on a plane and rendered to Syria for interrogation under torture.[58]

From more or less the outset, the United States indicated that it was their intention to send Maher not to his home in Canada but to Syria, a country where he had good reason to fear he would be tortured, especially if he were handed over to Syrian security services as a suspected terrorist. The United States also knew that this would happen. For at least the past ten years, the U.S. Department of State, Amnesty International, and Human Rights Watch have each documented torture at the hands of the Syrian Security services as routine.

Under torture, Maher was primarily interrogated about his relationship with certain individuals he had met casually while in Canada. He was asked about people and meetings that Syrian officials could never have known about, the very same people and meetings that had been the focus of Maher's interrogation in the United States. The only reasonable explanation is that the information was given to the Syrian government by the United States when the United States farmed out Maher's interrogation to the Syrians. The Syrian ambassador in Washington, D.C., the highest-ranking Syrian official in the United States, admitted as much; during a CBS *60 Minutes II* interview he stated that the Syrian government had taken Maher as a favor to the Americans and that they had cooperated with the United States throughout his detention, by sharing the information they gleaned from him under interrogation.[59]

After a year of investigation, the Syrians eventually released Maher from custody. They did so as a favor to the Canadians and because after an exhaustive investigation into his background they could not find a shred of evidence connecting him to al Qaeda or any other terrorist organization. The Syrian government released Maher back to Canada as an innocent man, and that is how his home country accepted him, yet the United States continues to insist that he is a hardened al Qaeda operative.

Maher is now seeking to clear his name, and has tirelessly and successfully campaigned in Canada for a full public inquiry into his removal from the United States. He is also speaking out against the practice of rendition to ensure that no one else suffers the same fate as he did. Maher's story demonstrates the futility of the U.S. government's rendition policy; what did it achieve in Maher's case apart from the destruction of an innocent man's life?

Sadly, Maher's case is not unique. Late one night in January 2003, the Center for Constitutional Rights took a call from Egypt from an Egyptian citizen who, after bad legal advice and a bungled immigration proceeding, had been rendered from the United States to interrogation and torture in Egypt. In halting English, Mohammed El-Zaher struggled to recount how in December 2003, after over nine months of detention in a jail in New Jersey, he was flown on a plane to Cairo accompanied by two immigration officials and physically handed over by them to officers from Egyptian State Security. With not a shred of evidence to support their allegations, the United States handed Mohammed over as a suspected terrorist.

Egyptian State Security then held Mohammed incommunicado for three months, interrogating and torturing him repeatedly. They subjected him to electroshock treatment, beatings, verbal abuse, death threats, and even more extreme forms of physical torture. The interrogation focused on his alleged membership in al Qaeda and his involvement in terrorist activities in the United States. Mohammed was not a member of al Qaeda and he knew nothing about terrorist organizations in the United States or elsewhere. He couldn't provide them with anything they did not already know. What caused Egyptian State Security to pursue this line of interrogation? We will likely never know the definitive answer to this question.

Mohammed endured torture for over three months before his elder brother, a senior member in the Egyptian military, tracked him down, pulled some strings, and secured his release from his rat-infested cell. After his release, Mohammed was compelled to check in with State Security on a weekly basis and account for his every move. In regular telephone calls to the Center for Constitutional Rights, Mohammed described how he was in constant fear for his life while he remained in Egypt. Eventually Mohammed made the difficult decision to flee his home, leaving his family and friends behind to seek asylum in Switzerland.

THE USE OF TORTURE, "STRESS AND DURESS," AND RENDITION: A LEGAL ANALYSIS

The prohibitions against torture and other cruel, inhuman, or degrading treatment are incorporated in every international human rights treaty as well as numerous international instruments such as the United Nations Declaration of Human Rights.[60] These prohibitions also form part of customary international human rights law and are explicitly recognized under U.S. domestic law.

The Convention Against Torture and Other Cruel, Inhuman, or Degrading Treatment or Punishment (CAT), a treaty ratified by the United States on October 21, 1994, includes the most comprehensive definition of torture under international law, defining it as "any act by which severe pain or suffering, whether physical or mental, is intentionally inflicted on a person ... by or at the instigation of or with the consent or acquiescence of a public official or other person acting in an official capacity."[61] CAT further obligates states to take action to prevent "other acts of cruel, inhuman, or degrading punishment which do not amount to acts of torture...."[62] Under CAT, member states are obligated to take steps, including the enactment of legislation, to eradicate torture within their territories. Article 2 (2) of CAT also establishes that the prohibition against torture is absolute: "no exceptional circumstances whatsoever," including a state of war, terrorist threats, or any other public emergency may be invoked to justify torture.

The International Covenant on Civil and Political Rights (ICCPR), ratified by the United States on September 8, 1992, contains similar prohibitions against torture and cruel, inhuman, or degrading treatment. Specifically, Article 7 provides that "[n]o one shall be subjected to torture or to cruel, inhuman, or degrading treatment or punishment." Like CAT, these prohibitions cannot be lifted for any reason, including war, terrorist threats, or other states of emergency.[63]

Conceptually, international law distinguishes between treatment that constitutes torture and that which constitutes inhuman or degrading treatment or punishment. The highly respected European Court of Human Rights, for example, in the case of *Ireland v. United Kingdom*,[64] elaborates upon this distinction. The Court found that the difference between torture and inhuman or degrading treatment is based on the intensity of the suffering inflicted. Torture is a severe form of cruel and inhuman treatment. The Court suggested that the distinction between the two is generated by a special "stigma" attached to torture, restricted to those acts of "deliberate inhuman treatment causing very serious and cruel suffering."[65] Adopting this reasoning, the European Court found that the use of five interrogation techniques by the UK military against suspected members of the IRA, including wall-standing, hooding, subjection to noise, sleep deprivation, and deprivation of food and water, constitute inhuman or degrading treatment but not torture. However, if these same acts were deliberately inflicted and carefully planned before being administered, with the express purpose of obtaining admissions or information from the victims, then they might well constitute acts of torture.[66] Moreover, today, some twenty-five years after its decision in *Ireland v. United Kingdom*, the European Court may consider these very same acts in and of themselves torture. In a decision from 1999, *Selmouni v. France*,[67] the Court sensibly found that definitions of torture and inhuman or degrading treatment should be interpreted in light of present-day conditions, so that certain acts once classified as the lesser "inhuman and degrading treatment," as opposed to "torture," could be classified differently in the future. Thus, the treatment meted out to the Irish terrorist suspects in the 1970s, such as prolonged hooding and other forms of sensory deprivation, could, under society's current and advancing standards of decency, constitute torture and not simply inhuman or degrading treatment.

A similar distinction between these differing forms of mistreatment is drawn by the United Nations Human Rights Committee, the body established to monitor and enforce compliance with the ICCPR. The Committee hears complaints brought by individuals worldwide. In *Vuolanne v. Finland*, for example, the Committee found that the determination of whether an Article 7 violation has occurred requires an assessment of all the circumstances of the case, "such as the duration and manner of the treatment, its physical or mental effects as well as the sex, age, and state of health of the victim."[68]

Following the above analysis, although many of the "stress and duress" interrogation methods adopted by the U.S. military may only constitute inhuman or degrading treatment when applied in isolation, they could very well meet the higher torture standard when administered together to persons detained incommunicado.

International bodies have identified specific acts that constitute torture. The Human Rights Committee, for example, has found that beatings, forced standing for long periods of time, and holding persons incommunicado for prolonged periods constitute torture and cruel, inhuman, or degrading treatment in violation of Article 7 and 10(1) of the ICCPR.[69] Importantly, the committee has noted that

> The [ICCPR] does not contain any definition of the concepts covered by Article 7 [prohibition against torture], nor does the Committee consider it necessary to

draw up a prohibited list of prohibited acts or to establish sharp distinctions between the different kinds of punishment or treatment; the distinctions depend on the nature, purpose and severity of the treatment applied.[70]

As noted, many of the detainees in U.S. control are held by the United States at undisclosed locations or virtually incommunicado at facilities such as Guantánamo. Under international law, such detention may in and of itself constitute torture. For example, in *El Megreisi v. Libya*, the Human Rights Committee found "prolonged incommunicado detention in an unknown location" to be "torture and cruel, inhuman treatment in violation of Articles 7 and 10(1)." In this case, the individual had effectively "disappeared," having been detained by Libyan security police for three years in unacknowledged detention before his wife was allowed to visit him. His subsequent location is unknown. Sir Nigel Rodley, the former United Nations special rapporteur on torture, a mechanism established by the United Nations Commission on Human Rights specifically to address the issue of torture, has said that this case stands for the proposition that prolonged incommunicado detention in itself can violate Article 7, even to the extent of constituting torture. Rodley suggests that the underlying logic of the committee's position is that the detention of persons in circumstances that give them or others grounds for fearing serious threat to their physical or mental integrity violates Article 7.[71] Similarly, the Inter-American Court on Human Rights has held that

prolonged isolation and deprivation of communication are in themselves cruel and inhuman treatment, harmful to the psychological and moral integrity of the person and a violation of the right of any detainee to respect for his inherent dignity as a human being. Such treat-

> ment, therefore, violates Article 5 of the [American] Convention on Human Rights [prohibition against torture, etc.].[72]

Among the specific acts listed by the United Nations special rapporteur on torture as constituting torture are "exposure to excessive light and noise ... prolonged denial of rest or sleep ... total isolation and sensory deprivation, being held in constant uncertainty in terms of space and time...."[73]

The prohibitions against torture and cruel, inhuman, or degrading treatment are also incorporated in every regional human rights treaty,[74] including, importantly, the American Declaration on the Rights and Duties of Man (American Declaration), which imposes binding international obligations on the United States.[75] In its recent *Report on Terrorism and Human Rights*, the Inter-American Commission on Human Rights cites a number of specific examples of acts committed in the context of interrogation that constitute inhuman treatment, including prolonged incommunicado detention, and keeping detainees hooded and naked in cells.

Not only does international human rights law absolutely prohibit the use of torture or other cruel or inhuman treatment, so too does international humanitarian law (IHL), the law applicable during armed conflict. As the United States views all aspects of its fight against al Qaeda, from Afghanistan to mainland United States, as an armed conflict rather than a criminal law enforcement operation, the rules of IHL as well as international human rights law need to be considered in assessing U.S. actions. Importantly, the right to humane treatment and the prohibition of torture apply equally in times of peace as well as war. Explicit prohibitions against the use of torture and other inhuman treatment of persons detained during wartime are incorporated in all the major international humanitarian law instruments, including the

Geneva Conventions, which the United States has ratified.[76] These same prohibitions also form part of customary international humanitarian law. Significantly, the prohibitions apply regardless of the legal status of the detainee. They cover interned civilians[77] as well as all captured combatants, whether they are prisoners of war,[78] unprivileged combatants,[79] or the newly created Bush administration category of "enemy combatant." Indeed, the willful torture or inhuman treatment of prisoners of war or other detainees also constitutes a "grave breach" of the Geneva Conventions—a war crime.[80]

The prohibitions against torture and other cruel, inhuman, and degrading treatment or punishment have long been recognized by all three branches of the U.S. government. Significantly, the United States has ratified both CAT and the ICCPR, which, as noted above, both expressly prohibit the use of torture or other cruel, inhuman, or degrading treatment. In its *Initial Report to the United Nations Committee Against Torture*, the U.S. Department of State, the body designated responsible under CAT for monitoring member state compliance with the treaty, stated:

> Torture is prohibited by law throughout the United States. It is categorically denounced as a matter of policy and as a tool of state authority. . . . No official of the government, federal, state or local, civilian or military is authorized to commit or to instruct anyone else to commit torture. Nor may any official condone or tolerate torture in any form. . . . U.S. law contains no provision permitting otherwise prohibited acts of torture or other cruel, inhuman or degrading treatment or punishment to be employed on grounds of exigent circumstances (for example, during a "state of public emergency") or on the orders from a superior officer or public authority.[81]

Among the acts singled out in the report as amounting to cruel, inhuman, or degrading treatment are substandard prison conditions, sexual abuse, and non-consensual medical and scientific experimentation.[82]

The United States has gone further than many other states in implementing legislation to give domestic effect to obligations it assumed through its ratification of CAT. For example, in 1991, Congress enacted the Torture Victim Protection Act, imposing civil liability for acts of torture perpetrated under "color of foreign law" anywhere in the world. Additionally, in 1994, Congress also passed legislation imposing criminal liability for torture wherever it occurs.[83]

Congress has also adopted legislation that gives express recognition to the prohibition against cruel, inhuman, or degrading treatment, including:

- 7 U.S.C. § 1733—prohibiting the provision of agricultural commodities to countries that practice cruel, inhuman, and degrading treatment
- 22 U.S.C. § 262d(a)(1)—stating that it is U.S. policy to avoid providing international assistance to countries that practice cruel, inhuman, or degrading treatment
- 22 U.S.C. § 2151n—prohibiting development assistance to countries that practice cruel, inhuman, or degrading treatment
- 22 U.S.C § 2304—prohibiting security assistance to countries that practice cruel, inhuman, or degrading treatment

And, in its annual reports on the human rights practices of countries worldwide, the U.S. Department of State devotes a whole section to an analysis of each country's resort to cruel, inhuman, or degrading treatment or punishment.[84]

A long line of judicial authority also recognizes the absolute prohibitions against torture and other forms of cruel, inhuman, or degrading treatment. For example, in *Filartega v. Pena-Irala*,[85] a court of appeals found that "an act of torture committed by a state official against one held in detention violates established norms of the international law of human rights and hence the law of nations." Since at least 1995, numerous courts have likewise found that cruel, inhuman, or degrading treatment violates international law. In *Xuncax v. Gramajo*,[86] the court held there to be a clear international prohibition against cruel, inhuman, or degrading treatment. Similarly, in *Wiwa v. Royal Dutch Petroleum Co.*,[87] a district court in New York found that "[t]he international prohibition against 'cruel, inhuman, or degrading treatment' is as universal as the proscriptions against torture...."

INTERNATIONAL HUMAN RIGHTS AND HUMANITARIAN LAW PROHIBITS THE RENDITION OF DETAINEES TO COUNTRIES WHERE THERE IS A SUBSTANTIAL RISK THAT THEY WILL BE SUBJECTED TO TORTURE

Not only is the United States responsible for the humane treatment of persons in its custody and control, it also has continuing responsibility for their treatment prior to and after transferring them to the custody of another state. Governments violate the prohibition against torture not only when they use torture directly, but also when they are complicit in torture committed by another state. Governments also violate the prohibition against torture when they "render" a person to a country where there is a substantial likelihood that person will be tortured or mistreated—a practice known under international law as *refoulment*.[88]

The prohibition against "rendering" persons to countries that practice torture is incorporated in international human rights instruments. CAT, for example, as well as prohibiting torture and mistreatment, prohibits member states, such as the United States, from sending persons to countries where it is known that such practices are likely to occur. Specifically, Article 3 of CAT provides:

> 1. No State Party shall expel, return ("refouler") or extradite a person to another State where there are substantial grounds for believing that he would be in danger of being subject to torture.

> 2. For the purpose of determining whether there are such grounds, the competent authorities shall take into account all relevant considerations including, where applicable, the existence in the State concerned of a consistent pattern of gross, flagrant, or mass violations of human rights.[89]

The prohibition of rendition is also incorporated in Article XXVII of the American Declaration on the Rights and Duties of Man, a regional human rights instrument, which, like CAT and the ICCPR, imposes binding international obligations on the United States. The Inter-American Commission on Human Rights, the body responsible for the enforcement of the American Declaration, has found that a state that expels, returns, or extradites a person to another state when there are substantial grounds for believing the person might be subjected to torture will be considered responsible for violating that person's right to personal security or humane treatment.[90] Likewise, the European Court of Human Rights has found that the prohibition against returning or expelling a person to a state that practices torture remains absolute, "irrespective of the victim's conduct."[91]

In partial fulfillment of its undertakings under CAT, the United States has enacted legislation prohibiting the transfer of persons to countries where they would be subjected to torture. The Foreign Affairs Reform and Restructuring Act of 1998 (FARRA) provides:

> It shall be the policy of the United States not to expel, extradite, or otherwise effect the involuntary return of any person to a country in which there are substantial grounds for believing the person would be in danger of being subjected to torture, regardless of whether the person is physically present in the United States.[92]

FARRA also requires relevant government agencies to promulgate and enforce regulations to implement CAT. To date, in accordance with this policy, only the Department of Justice and Department of State have passed such regulations.

In letters to Human Rights Watch dated April 2, 2003, and to Senator Patrick J. Leahy dated June 25, 2003, William J. Haynes II, general counsel of the Department of Defense, noted that it was the policy of the United States to comply with all of its legal obligations in the treatment of detainees, including its obligations under CAT. In addition, Mr. Haynes stated that "[i]f the war on terrorists of global reach requires transfers of detained enemy combatants to other countries for continued detention on our behalf, U.S. government instructions are to obtain appropriate assurances that such enemy combatants are not tortured," adding that the United States does not "expel, return ('*refouler*') or extradite individuals to other countries where the U.S. believes it is 'more likely than not' that they will be tortured."[93]

An examination of U.S. Department of State annual reports on human rights practices ("Department of State reports"), as well as reports by major human rights organizations such as Amnesty International and Human Rights Watch, reveal that the United States is fully aware of the occurrence of torture and other cruel, inhuman, or degrading treatment in countries—including Egypt, Jordan, and Syria—to which it has "rendered" persons under its control.

For example, the 2002 Department of State report on Egypt—the country to which the United States "rendered" Mohammed El-Zaher—notes that "there were numerous, credible reports that security forces tortured and mistreated citizens."

> Principal methods of torture employed by the police, as reported by victims, included: Being stripped and blind-folded; suspended from a ceiling or doorframe with feet just touching the floor; beaten with fists, whips, metal rods, or other objects; subjected to electrical shocks; and doused with cold water. Victims frequently report being subjected to threats and forced to sign blank papers to be used against the victim or the victim's family in the future should the victim complain of abuse. Some victims, including male and female detainees, reported that they were sexually assaulted or threatened with the rape of themselves or family members.[94]

In its 2003 country report on Egypt, Amnesty International reports that "[t]orture continues to be widespread in detention centers throughout the country. The UN Special Rapporteur on torture also concluded that 'torture is systematically practiced by the security forces in Egypt, in particular by State Security Intelligence.'"[95]

The 2002 Department of State report on Jordan, Maher Arar's first port of call before his yearlong detention in Syria, notes that

> police and security forces sometimes abuse detainees physically and verbally during detention and interrogation, and allegedly also use torture. . . . The most frequently alleged methods of torture include sleep deprivation, beatings on the soles of the feet, prolonged suspension with ropes in contorted positions, and

extended solitary confinement. Defendants in high-pro-
file cases before the State Security Court claimed to have
been subjected to physical and psychological abuse
while in detention.[96]

Likewise in Jordan, Amnesty International observes that
"[r]eports continue to be received of torture and ill-treatment by
members of the security forces and prison services."[97]

Finally, the 2002 State Department Report for Syria notes that

there was credible evidence that security forces continued to use torture, although to a lesser extent than in
previous years. Former prisoners and detainees report
that torture methods include administering electrical
shocks; pulling out fingernails; forcing objects into the
rectum; beating, sometimes while the victim is suspended from the ceiling; hyper-extending the spine; and
using a chair that bends backwards to asphyxiate the victim or fracture the victim's spine.

Further, "Although torture occurs in prisons, torture is most
likely to occur while detainees are being held at one of the many
detention centers run by the various security services throughout
the country, and particularly while the authorities are attempting
to extract a confession or information regarding an alleged crime
or alleged accomplices."[98] Amnesty International reported that
"torture and ill-treatment continued to be inflicted routinely on
political prisoners...."[99]

From the cases noted above it seems abundantly clear that renditions have taken place both from the United States and from
outside this country's borders that violate U.S. obligations under
CAT, its own domestic law, and its own policy guidelines as
detailed most recently by William J. Haynes II.

Over the past two and half years, the United States has routinely rendered individuals as terrorist suspects to governments, such as those of Egypt, Jordan, and Syria, that have a very long track record of subjecting detainees to torture and other cruel, inhuman, or degrading treatment. For at least the past ten years, for example, Department of State reports note that the Syrian security forces subject criminal suspects to interrogation under torture. Any individual sent by the United States into the arms of the Syrian security forces as a suspected terrorist would "more likely than not" be subjected to torture. Yet, this is precisely where the United States sent Maher Arar.

Government agencies involved in renditions have sought to hide behind diplomatic assurances obtained from the relevant country that the individual rendered will not be subjected to torture.[100] However, one must seriously question whether assurances from countries with a history of human rights abuses, condemned in Department of State reports, can ever adequately fulfill U.S. obligations not to render persons within its control to such countries. It is naive to believe that a mere promise of proper treatment will adequately protect against routine torture and ill-treatment. Such assurances would not be worth the paper on which they were written.

CONCLUSION

The prohibition against torture and other cruel, inhuman, or degrading treatment, as well as the prohibition against rendition to countries that torture, rank among some of the most fundamental human rights. Not only do these prohibitions form an integral part of the international framework of human rights protections, they have also been incorporated into U.S. domestic law. Yet, in the "war on terrorism" there is a growing body of evidence that these once sacrosanct protections are being thrown to the four winds by the

United States, the world's only superpower and a leading advocate for the expansion of human rights and democracy worldwide.

This flagrant disregard of fundamental international standards is causing serious and possibly irreversible damage to this country's credibility, thereby making it increasingly difficult to build the international coalitions now vital to tackle the world's problems; struggles like the "war on terrorism" cannot possibly be "won" by the United States, powerful as it may be, acting alone.

President Bush has said that he wants to lead the fight against terrorism "by example." It is becoming increasingly apparent, however, that the example being set by the United States is a bad one. Less powerful countries will look to the United States' violations of human rights as a basis for justifying the violations of the rights of their own nationals. And finally, as history amply demonstrates, adoption of harsh and oppressive measures by a state to tackle perceived threats to national security do not result in a decrease in lawless activity. Rather, such tactics oftentimes lead to a corresponding increase in violence. For example, the counterterrorism measures adopted by the UK against suspected IRA terrorists in Northern Ireland in the 1970s, including methods of interrogation almost identical to United States' "stress and duress" techniques, resulted in a manifold rise in IRA membership and, in addition, some of the worst attacks against civilian targets witnessed in the decades-long civil conflict.

The systemic use of torture by the French military on suspected members of the Algerian liberation movement (FLN) during the eight-year-long Algerian war (1954–62) was similarly unsuccessful in countering attacks against the civilian population of that country. Nor has the use of military might and torture ended the violence in Israel; in fact it seems to have fomented it. The United States, through the employment of torture and rendition in execution of its "war against terrorism" would appear to have learned little from the mistakes of the past.

To bring an end to the scourge of terrorism it will require a much more sophisticated approach than the one presently adopted; bombs, arbitrary detention, and torture are simply not working. A more effective approach would be one that embraces, as a bare minimum, respect for the rule of law and recognition of fundamental civil and human rights protections for everyone, regardless of national origin, skin color, or religious affiliation.

NOTES

1   *See, e.g.,* U.S. Department of Defense News Briefing (January 30, 2002) per Secretary of Defense Rumsfeld: "There's thousands of these people that are being held by the Afghans, they're being held by the Afghans, they're being held by the Pakistanis, they're being held by us. . . . And as we go through and look at them, we're . . . trying to sort out the al Qaeda and the more senior Taliban." Cited in Amnesty International, Memorandum on the Rights of People in U.S Custody in Afghanistan and Guantánamo Bay, April 15, 2002, 17.

2   Ibid.

3   *See* John Mintz, "Al Qaeda Interrogations Fall Short of the Mark," *Washington Post,* April 21, 2002; Eric Schmitt, "Ideas and Trends: There Are Ways To Make Them Talk," *New York Times,* June 16, 2002; Greg Miller, "Intelligence Officers Read Between the Enemy Lines," *Los Angeles Times,* June 23, 2002.

4   *See, e.g.,* Article 15-6 Investigation of the 800th Military Police Brigade by Maj. Gen. Antonio M. Taguba. Available at: http://www.globalsecurity.org/intell/library/reports/2004/800-mp-bde.htm. *See also* Report of the International Committee of the Red Cross (ICRC) on the Treatment by the Coalition Forces of Prisoners of War and Other Protected Persons by the Geneva Conventions in Iraq During Arrest, Internment and Interrogation (February 2004). Available at: http://www.globalsecurity.org/military/library/report/2004/icrc_report_iraq_feb2004.pdf .

5   President Bush and other U.S. officials have stated that 3,000 individuals had been detained as of December 2002. *See* Dana Priest and Barton Gellman, "U.S. Decries Abuse But Defends Interrogations"; "'Stress and Duress' Tactics Used on Terrorism Suspects Held in Secret Overseas Facilities," *Washington Post,* December 26, 2002.

6   Priest and Gellman, "U.S. Decries Abuse"; *See also* Remarks by Secretary of State Colin Powell to the U.N. Security Council re: Iraq's Weapons of Mass Destruction, Federal News Service, Inc., February 6, 2003; and Patrick E. Tyler, "Intelligence Break Led U.S. to Tie Envoy Killing to Iraq Qaeda Cell," *New York Times,* February 6, 2003).

7   On July 30, 2004, the first Guantánamo detainee was brought before a Combatant Status Review Tribunal, described in chapter 2. These military tribunals are not courts and do not provide due process.

8   *See* statement of U.S. national security spokesman, Sean McCormack, quoted in Priest and Gellman, "U.S. Decries Abuse."

9   *See, e.g.,* Molly Moore, "Villagers Released by American Troops Say They Were Beaten, Kept in 'Cage,'" *Washington Post,* February 11, 2002; Carlotta Gall, "Released Afghans Tell of Beatings," *New York Times* February 11, 2002 (Villagers mistakenly identified by U.S. forces as Taliban or al Qaeda members, claimed that during a raid on Uruzgan village they had their hands and feet tied, were blindfolded, and hooded and flown to the U.S. base at Kandahar. They claim to have been beaten and otherwise physically assaulted upon arrival at the base. One boy claimed that he was kept in solitary confinement in a shipping container for eight days.). *See also* John Ward, "Afghans Falsely Held by U.S. Tried to Explain," *Washington Post,* March 26, 2002; "Afghans Say U.S. Troops Abused Them," Associated Press, March 23, 2002. (During a raid on compound near Kandahar, villagers claimed to have their hands and feet bound, hands tied and black hoods placed over their heads while being beaten by U.S. troops. Thirty four of them taken into custody alleged that they were assaulted and held in tiny cages.) There was an investigation carried out by U.S. military in to the Uruzgan allegations, but the results of these investigations were inconclusive on a number of fronts. *See generally* Amnesty International, Memorandum on the Rights of People in U.S Custody in Afghanistan and Guantánamo Bay, April 15, 2002.

10 Priest and Gellman, "U.S. Decries Abuse." *See also* Duncan Campbell, "U.S. Interrogators Turn to 'Torture Lite'" *The Guardian* (London), January 25, 2003.

11 Priest and Gellman, "U.S. Decries Abuse."

12 *See also,* Paul Harris and Burhan Wazir, "Al Qaeda Suspect Is Starved of Food and Sleep at Army Base Where Two Have Died," *Observer* (London), December 29, 2002 (reporting that the parents of British citizen Moazzam Begg, who has been detained at the U.S. military base in Bagram since his arrest at the end of 2001, had received a letter in which he complained of hunger and of being kept awake by bright lights).

13 David Ensor, "U.S. Officials: 'Inaccuracies' in Reports of Tough Interrogations," CNN, December 27, 2002; *See also* "Ends, Means and Barbarity—Torture—The Use and Abuse of Torture," *Economist* (London), January 11, 2003 (describing the report as "well documented" and seeing "little reason to doubt [its] veracity").

14 Available at: http://www.hrw.org/press/2002/12/us1227.htm.

15 Letter from William J. Haynes II, General Counsel of the Department of Defense, to Kenneth Roth, Executive Director, Human Rights Watch (April 2, 2003). Available at: http://www.hrw.org/press/2003/04/dodltr040203.pdf

16 Secretary of State for Defense Rumsfeld, Department of Defense News Transcript (March 21, 2002).

17 John Mintz, "R.I. Guard Relieves a Top Officer, General, Head of MPs at Guantánamo Bay, Clashed with Detainee Interrogators,"*Washington Post,* October 16, 2002 (reporting that the general clashed repeatedly with the head of the camp's interrogation unit and "raised questions about some of the tactics of psychological pressure that interrogators sometimes used on prisoners").

18 Joe Conason, "Gin-Mill Justice for John Walker?" *New York Observer,* December 16, 2001.

19 Ibid.

20 *United States v. Lindh,* plea agreement (July 15, 2002).

21 Memorandum for White House Counsel, Alberto R. Gonzales from Assistant Attorney General Jay S. Bybee, *Re: Application of Treaties and Laws to al Qaeda and Taliban Detainees* (January 22, 2002) Memorandum for Alberto R. Gonzales Counsel to the President from Assistant Attorney General Jay S. Bybee, *Re: Status of Taliban Forces Under Article 4 of the Third Geneva Convention of 1949* (February 7, 2002)

22 Memorandum for Alberto Gonzales, Counsel to the President, from Jay S. Bybee, Assistant Attorney General, Re: Standards of conduct for interrogation under 18 U.S.C. §§ 2340–2340A (August 1, 2002).

23 Michael Hirsh, et al., "A Tortured Debate," *Newsweek*, June 21, 2004.

24 Carlotta Gall, "U.S. Military Investigating Death of Afghan in Custody," *New York Times*, March 4, 2003; Eric Lichtblau and Adam Liptak, "Questioning of Accused Expected to be Humane, Legal and Aggressive," *New York Times,* March 4, 2003.

25 Gall, "U.S. Military Investigating Death."

26 Ibid.

27 Lichtblau and Liptak, "Questioning of Accused."

28 Ibid.

29 Don Van Natta Jr., "Questioning Terror Suspects in a Dark and Surreal World," *New York Times*, March 9, 2003.

30 James Risen, David Johnston and Neil A Lewis, "Harsh C.I.A. Methods Cited in Top Qaeda Interrogations," *New York Times,* May 13, 2004.

31 Gall, "U.S. Military Investigating Death," *New York Times,* March 4, 2003; Marc Kaufman, "Army Probing Deaths of Two Afghan Prisoners," Washington Post, March 5, 2003.

32 Letter to Senator Patrick Leahy from William J. Haynes II, General Counsel of the Department of Defense, June 25, 2003.

33 Douglas Jehl and David Rohde, "Afghan Deaths Linked to Unit at Iraq Prison," *New York Times* May 24, 2004.

34 Terry Frieden, "U.S. Indicts CIA Contractor in Afghanistan Prison Death," CNN.com, June 22, 2004.

35 Priest and Gellman, "U.S. Decries Abuse."

36 Ibid.

37 Robert Baer, *See No Evil: The True Story of a Ground Soldier in the CIAs War on Terrorism* (New York: Three Rivers Press, 2003). *See also* BBC Three interview with Robert Baer. Available at: http://www.bbc.co.uk/bbcthree/tv/third_degree/stars_stripes_interview.shtml.

38 Priest and Gellman, "U.S. Decries Abuse."

39 Stephen Grey, "America's Gulag," *New Statesman* (London), May 17, 2004.

40 Rajiv Chandrasekaran and Peter Finn, "U.S. Behind Secret Transfer of Terror Suspects," *The Washington Post,* March 11, 2002. *See also* "Scores of Al-Qa'ida Arab Prisoners Reportedly Flown to Egypt, Jordan," BBC, citing text of a report carried in Jordanian newspaper, *Al-Majid* on April 1, 2002.

41 Ibid.

42 "Pakistan Trying to Identify al Qaeda Suspects, No Extradition Plans Yet," Agence France Presse, January 11, 2003 (reporting that 420 al Qaeda suspects have been rendered by Pakistan to the United States since September 11, 2001).

43 Kareem Fahim, "The Invisible Men," *The Village Voice*, March 30, 2004.

44 U.S. Government Response to Inter-American Commission on Human Rights Request for Precautionary Measures (April 18, 2002).

45 *See* Letter from Gareth Peirce of Birnberg Peirce & Partners to Center for Constitutional Rights, March 4, 2003 (copy on file with author).

46 *See* Letter from Gareth Peirce of Birnberg Peirce & Partners, Solicitors to UK Foreign Secretary, Foreign and Commonwealth Office, London, January 31, 2003 (copy on file with author); Affidavit of Solicitor Gareth Peirce in *El-Banna v. Bush*, civil action No. 04-CV-144 (RWR) DDC 2004); *See also* Amnesty International Urgent Action, UA 359/02, AI Index: AFR 27/006/2002 (December 11, 2002); "Human Rights Forgotten in U.S.A.'s 'War on terrorism,'" Amnesty International, March 2003; "Al Qaeda Suspects Arrested in the Gambia," *Independent*, Banjul, December 23, 2002.

47 Amnesty International, United States of America: The Threat of a Bad Example (August 2003).

48 Swedish TV4 Kalla Fakta program: *The Broken Promise*, May 17, 2004. Transcript available at: http://www.statewatch.org/news/2004/may/Sweden.pdf

49 Ibid.

50 Craig Whitlock, "A Secret Deportation of Terror Suspects," *Washington Post*, July 25, 2004.

51 Ibid.

52 *See Begg v. Bush*, Civil Action No. 04-CV-1137 (RMC).

53 "Fears for Bagram Detainee: Briton Says He Was Kept In The Dark For A Year By Americans," *The Guardian* (London) (February 13, 2003).

54 Supra n.52

55 *See Habub v. Bush*, Civil Action No. 02-CV-1130 (CKK).

56 Ibid.

57 *See, e.g.*, Daniel J. Wakin, "Tempers Flare After U.S. Sends a Canadian Citizen Back to Syria on Terror Suspicions," New York Times, November 11, 2002.

58 *See Maher Arar v. Ashcroft et al.* 04-CV-249 (DGT) (E.D.N.Y. Jan. 22, 2004). Complaint available at: http://www.ccr-ny.org/v2/legal/september_11th/docs/ArarComplaint.pdf.

59 "His Year in Hell," *60 Minutes II*, CBS, January 21, 2004.

60 *See* Universal Declaration of Human Rights, G.A. res. 217A (III), art. 5, U.N. Doc A/810 at 71 (1948); International Covenant on Civil and Political Rights, G.A. res. 2200A (XXI), 21 U.N. GAOR Supp. (No. 16) at 52, art. 7, U.N. Doc. A/6316 (1966), 999 U.N.T.S. 171, entered into force March 23, 1976 (ICCPR); Convention Against Torture and Other Cruel, Inhuman or Degrading Treatment or Punishment (CAT), G.A. res. 39/46, annex, 39 U.N. GAOR Supp. (No. 51) at 197, U.N. Doc. A/39/51 (1984), entered into force June 26, 1987; Declaration on the Protection of All Persons from Being Subjected to Torture and Other Cruel, Inhuman or Degrading Treatment or Punishment, G.A. res. 3452 (XXX), annex, 30 U.N. GAOR Supp. (No. 34) at 91, U.N. Doc. A/10034 (1975).

61 CAT, art. 1.

62 CAT, art. 16(2).

63 ICCPR, Art. 4.

64 2 E.H.R.R. 25 (1979).

65 Ibid. at ¶ 167.

66 *See, e.g., Aksoy v. Turkey*, 23 E.H.R.R. 553 (1997) (finding that stripping a detainee with arms tied behind his back and suspending him by his arms constitutes torture).

67 29 E.H.R.R. 403 (1999) at ¶ 422.

68 Human Rights Committee Sess. 44, Comm. No. 265/1987, U.N. Doc. Supp. No. 40 (A/44/40) (1989).

69 *Bouton v. Uruguay* (3711978), Report of the Human Rights Committee, *GAOR*, 36th Session, Supp. No. 40 (1981), Annex XIV, ¶ 13. (Victim forced to stand for 35 hours, with minor interruptions; her wrists were bound with a strip of coarse cloth which hurt her and her eyes were continuously kept bandaged; she could hear the cries of other detainees being tortured; and she was verbally threatened [at ¶ 2.3]); *See also Birindwa and Tshisekedi v. Zaire* (241 and 242/1987), Report of the Human Rights Committee, Vol. II, GAOR, 45th Session, Supp. No. 40 (1990), Annex I, ¶ 13(b). (Victim "deprived of food and drink for four days after arrest" and kept under unacceptable sanitary conditions.) *See also Muteba v. Zaire* (124/1982), Report of the Human Rights Committee, UN Official Records of the General Assembly, 22nd Session, Supp. 40 (1984), Communication No. 124/1982, Democratic Republic of the Congo, 24/07/84. CCPR/C/22/D/124/1982, ¶ 10.2; *Setelich v. Uruguay* (63/1979), Report of Human Rights Committee, UN Official Records of the General Assembly, 14th Session, Communication No. 63/1979 : Uruguay. 28/10/81 CCPR/C/14/D/63/1979, ¶ 16.2; *Weinberger v. Uruguay* (28/1978), Report of the Human Rights Committee, UN Official Records of the General Assembly, 31st Session, Communication No. 28/1978, UN Doc. CCPR/C/11/D/28/1978, ¶ 12.

70 Report of the Human Rights Committee, UN Doc. A/47/40 (1990), Annex VI A, ¶ 4, general comment 20(44) replacing and reflecting upon general comment 7(16). *See also,* Report of the Human Rights Committee, GAOR, 37th Session Supp. 40 (1982), Annex V, general comment 7(16), ¶ 2.

71 Nigel S. Rodley, *The Treatment of Prisoners Under International Law* (London: Oxford, 1987), 349.

72 Inter-American Court of Human Rights, *Velasquez-Rodriguez* case, Judgment of July 29, 1988, Series C, No. 4, ¶¶ 156,187.

73 IACHR, *Report on Terrorism and Human Rights*, OEA/Ser.L/V/II.116 (2002) citing "Torture and other Cruel, Inhuman or Degrading Treatment or Punishment," Report of the Special Rapporteur, Mr. P. Kooijmans, appointed pursuant to Commission on Human Rights res. 1985/33 E/CN.4/1986/15, February 19, 1986, ¶ 119.

74 African Charter on Human and Peoples' Rights, June 27, 1981, art. 5, OAU Doc. CAB/LEG/67/3/Rev. 5 (1981); American Convention on Human Rights, O.A.S. Treaty Series No. 36, art. 5, 1144 U.N.T.S. 123 entered into force July 18, 1978, reprinted in Basic Documents Pertaining to Human Rights in the Inter-American System, OEA/Ser.L.V/II.82 doc.6 rev.1 at 25 (1992); Inter-American Convention to Prevent and Punish Torture, O.A.S. Treaty Series No. 67, entered into force February 28, 1987, reprinted in Basic Documents Pertaining to Human Rights in the Inter-American System, OEA/Ser.L.V/II.82 doc.6 rev.1 at 83 (1992); [European] Convention for the Protection of Human Rights and Fundamental Freedoms (ETS No. 5), 213 U.N.T.S. 222, entered into force September 3, 1953, as amended by Protocols Nos. 3, 5, and 8 which entered into

force on September 21, 1970, December 20, 1971 and January 1, 1990 respectively; European Convention for the Prevention of Torture and Inhuman or Degrading Treatment or Punishment, E.T.S. 126, entered into force February 1, 1989.

75 Under the Charter of the Organization of American States, a treaty ratified by the United States, the Inter-American Commission on Human Rights, a seven-member body of jurists based in Washington, D.C., are mandated to monitor and enforce member states' compliance with the American Declaration. *See* Decision on Request for Precautionary Measures (Detainees at Guantánamo Bay, Cuba), Inter-American Court of Human Rights (March 12, 2002) reprinted in 41 I.L.M. 532, 533 (2002).

76 *See* International Committee on the Red Cross, States Party to the Geneva Conventions and Their Additional Protocols. Available at: www.icrc.org.

77 Art. 32, Geneva Convention relative to the Protection of Civilian Persons in Time of War, 75 U.N.T.S. 287, art. 32, entered into force October 21, 1950 (Geneva IV).

78 Art., 17, Geneva Convention relative to the Treatment of Prisoners of War, 75 U.N.T.S. 135, art. 17, entered into force October 21, 1950 (Geneva III).

79 Art. 75, Protocol Additional to the Geneva Conventions of August 12, 1949, and relating to the Protection of Victims of International Armed Conflicts (Protocol I), art. 75, June 8, 1977; Common Article 3, Geneva Conventions.

80 In the War Crimes Act, U.S.C. 18 §2441, the United States has criminalized grave breaches of the Geneva Conventions.

81 U.S. Department of State, *Initial Report of the United States of America to the United Nations Committee Against Torture*, Introduction (1999).

82 Ibid. at ¶¶ 65–70.

83 18 U.S.C. § 2340A

84 U.S. Department of State country reports on human rights practices. Available at: http://www.state.gov/g/drl/hr/c1470.htm.

85 630 F.2d 876 (2d Cir. 1980).

86 886 F. Supp. 162, 187 (D. Mass. 1995).

87 2002 WL 319887, AT *8 (S.D.N.Y. 2002).

88 *See, e.g.*, arts. 3 and 4, Convention against Torture and Other Cruel, Inhuman or Degrading Treatment or Punishment (CAT), adopted December 10, 1984, 1465 U.N.T.S. 85 (entered into force June 26, 1987).

89 As with the prohibition against torture, the prohibition against rendition applies equally in times of peace or war. For example, similar provisions to those of article 3 of the CAT are included in article 12 of Geneva III, which prohibits a state party from making such transfers in relation to POWs.

90 IACHR, Report on Canada OEA/Ser.L./V/II.106 (2000) at ¶154.

91 *Chahal v. United Kingdom* (1997) 23 E.H.R.R. 413 at ¶ 1831.

92 *See* Pub. L. 105–277, div. G, Title XXII, 112 Stat. 2682–822 (Oct. 21, 1998).

93 http://www.hrw.org/press/2003/06tortureday.htm.

94 http://www.state.gov/g/drl/rls/hrrpt/2001/nea/8248.htm.

95 http://web.amnesty.org/web/ar2002.nsf/mde/egypt!Open.

96 http://www.state.gov/g/drl/rls/hrrpt/2001/nea/8266.htm.

97 http://web.amnesty.org/web/ar2002.nsf/mde/jordan!Open.

98 http://www.state.gov/g/drl/rls/hrrpt/2001/nea/8298.htm.
99 http://web.amnesty.org/web/ar2002.nsf/mde/syria!Open
100 Human Rights Watch, "'Empty Promises': Diplomatic Assurances No Safeguard Against Torture." Available at: http://www.hrw.org/reports/2004/un0404/

5
The Road to Abu Ghraib

Reed Brody

(Excerpted from a June 2004 Human Rights Watch report.)

SINCE LATE APRIL 2004, when the first photographs appeared of U.S. military personnel humiliating, torturing, and otherwise mistreating detainees at Abu Ghraib prison in Iraq, the U.S. government has repeatedly sought to portray the abuse as an isolated incident, the work of a few "bad apples" acting without orders. On May 4, U.S. Secretary of Defense Donald H. Rumsfeld, in a formulation that would be used over and over again by U.S. officials, described the abuses at Abu Ghraib as "an exceptional, isolated" case. In a nationally televised address on May 24, President George W. Bush spoke of "disgraceful conduct by a few American troops who dishonored our country and disregarded our values."

In fact, the only exceptional aspect of the abuse at Abu Ghraib may have been that it was photographed. As discussed in chapter 4, detainees in U.S. custody in Afghanistan have testified that they experienced treatment similar to what happened in Abu Ghraib— from beatings to prolonged sleep and sensory deprivation to being held naked—as early as 2002. Comparable—and, indeed, more extreme—cases of torture and inhuman treatment have been extensively documented by the International Committee of the Red Cross and by journalists at numerous locations in Iraq outside Abu Ghraib.

This pattern of abuse did not result from the acts of individual soldiers who broke the rules. It resulted from decisions (discussed in other chapters of this book) made by the Bush administration to bend, ignore, or cast rules aside.

It is not yet clear which techniques of ill-treatment or torture were formally approved at which levels of the U.S. government and the degree of severity allowed in their application, or whether they were informally encouraged. What is clear is that they were used systematically both in Afghanistan and then in Iraq, and that they were also used on some scale at Guantánamo. It is also clear that the purpose of these techniques is to inflict pain, suffering, and severe humiliation on detainees. It is not surprising that once that purpose was legitimized by military and intelligence officials, ordinary soldiers came to believe that even more extreme forms of abuse were acceptable. The brazenness with which some soldiers conducted themselves at Abu Ghraib, snapping photographs and flashing the "thumbs-up" sign as they abused prisoners, confirms that they felt they had nothing to hide from their superiors.

Until the publication of the Abu Ghraib photographs forced action, Bush administration officials took at best a "see no evil, hear no evil" approach to all reports of detainee mistreatment. From the earliest days of the war in Afghanistan and the occupation of Iraq, the U.S. government has been aware of allegations of abuse. Yet high-level pledges of humane treatment were never implemented with specific orders or guidelines to forbid coercive methods of interrogation. Investigations of deaths in custody languished; soldiers and intelligence personnel accused of abuse, including all cases involving the killing of detainees, escaped judicial punishment. When, in the midst of the worst abuses, the International Committee of the Red Cross complained to coalition forces, army officials apparently responded by trying to curtail the ICRC's access.

Concern for the basic rights of persons taken into custody in

Afghanistan and Iraq did not factor into the Bush administration's agenda. The administration largely dismissed expressions of concern for their treatment, from both within the government and without. This, too, sent a message to those dealing with detainees in the field about the priorities of those in command.

The severest abuses at Abu Ghraib occurred in the immediate aftermath of a decision by Secretary Rumsfeld to step up the hunt for "actionable intelligence" among Iraqi prisoners. The officer who oversaw intelligence gathering at Guantánamo was brought in to overhaul interrogation practices in Iraq, and teams of interrogators from Guantánamo were sent to Abu Ghraib. The commanding general in Iraq issued orders to "manipulate an internee's emotions and weaknesses." Military police were ordered by military intelligence to "set physical and mental conditions for favorable interrogation of witnesses." The captain who oversaw interrogations at the Afghan detention center where two prisoners died in detention posted "Interrogation Rules of Engagement" at Abu Ghraib, authorizing coercive methods (with prior written approval of the military commander)—such as the use of military guard dogs to instill fear—that violate the Geneva Conventions and the CAT.[1]

Unlike U.S. actions in the global campaign against terrorism, the armed conflict in Iraq was in part justified by the government as a way to help bring democracy and respect for the rule of law to an Iraqi population long-suffering under Saddam Hussein. Abusive treatment used against terrorism suspects after September 11 came to be considered permissible by the United States in an armed conflict to suppress resistance to a military occupation.

The Bush administration apparently believed that the new wars it was fighting could not be won if it was constrained by "old" rules. The disturbing information coming to light points to an official policy of torture and cruel, inhuman, or degrading treatment. The Bush administration has denied having a policy to torture or abuse detainees. Human Rights Watch calls on the administration to demonstrate conclusively that its public disavowal of torture and other mistreatment of detainees in U.S. custody reflects the actual policy of the U.S. government, and to make public all relevant government documents. The administration should also detail the steps being taken to ensure that these abusive practices do not continue, and to prosecute vigorously all those responsible for ordering or condoning this abuse.

Ironically, the administration is now finding that it may be losing the war for hearts and minds around the world precisely because it threw those rules out. Rather than advance the war on terror, the widespread prisoner abuse has damaged efforts to build global support for countering terrorism. Indeed, each new photo of an American soldier humiliating an Iraqi could be considered a recruiting poster for al Qaeda. Policies adopted to make the United States more secure from terrorism have in fact made it more vulnerable.

. . .

IRAQ: APPLYING COUNTERTERRORISM TACTICS DURING A MILITARY OCCUPATION

The United States, as an occupying power in Iraq under the Geneva Conventions, may deprive civilians in Iraq of their liberty in only two situations: for "imperative reasons of security" or for prosecution.[2] Since President Bush declared the end of major combat in Iraq in May 2003, more than 12,000 Iraqis have been taken into custody by U.S. forces and detained for weeks or months. Until very recently, the United States has failed to ensure that so-called security detainees received a proper review of their cases as is required under the Geneva Conventions.[3] In its February 2004 report to Coalition forces, the International Committee of the Red Cross reported that military intelligence officers told the ICRC that 70 to 90 percent of those in custody in Iraq in 2003 had been arrested by mistake.[4]

The United States' treatment of detainees in Iraq was shrouded in secrecy from the beginning of the occupation. What is clear is that abusive treatment used after September 11 on suspects in the "war on terror" came to be considered permissible in an armed conflict in order to suppress resistance to a military occupation. Procedures used in Afghanistan and Guantánamo were imported to Iraq, including the use of "stress and duress" tactics and the use of prison guards to set the conditions for the interrogation of detainees.[5]

In the aftermath of the Abu Ghraib scandal, information has come to light that suggests that harsh and coercive interrogation techniques such as subjecting detainees to painful stress positions and extended sleep deprivation have been routinely used in detention centers throughout Iraq. Department of Defense officials said that military intelligence "Human Exploitation Teams" regularly used so called "50/10 tactics": 50 minutes in sun with a bag over the head in stressful positions followed by 10 minutes of rest.[6]

In its February 2004 report, the ICRC found that "methods of physical and psychological coercion were used by the military intelligence in *a systematic way* to gain confessions and extract information" (emphasis added). The methods cited by the ICRC included:

- hooding to disorient and prevent detainees from breathing freely
- forcing detainees to remain for prolonged periods in painful stress positions
- attaching detainees to the bars of cell doors repeatedly over several days, for several hours each time, naked or in positions causing physical pain

- holding detainees naked in dark cells for several days and parading them naked, sometimes hooded or with women's underwear over their heads
- sleep, food, and water deprivation
- exposing detainees, while hooded, to the sun for prolonged periods during the hottest time of day

The classified investigative military report of Major General Antonio Taguba confirmed these findings. Taguba reported that "numerous incidents of sadistic, blatant, and wanton criminal abuses" were inflicted on several detainees. His catalogue was even longer than the ICRC's:

- punching, slapping, and kicking detainees; jumping on their naked feet
- videotaping and photographing naked male and female detainees
- forcibly arranging detainees in various sexually explicit positions for photographing
- forcing groups of male detainees to masturbate themselves while being photographed and videotaped
- arranging naked detainees in a pile and then jumping on them
- positioning a naked detainee on a box, with a sandbag on his head, and attaching wires to his fingers, toes, and penis to simulate electric torture
- writing "I am a Rapist" [sic] on the leg of a detainee alleged to have forcibly raped a 15-year-old fellow detainee, and then photographing him naked
- placing a dog chain or strap around a naked detainee's neck and having a female soldier pose with him for a picture
- male military police guard having sex with a female detainee[7]

- breaking chemical lights and pouring the phosphoric liquid on detainees
- threatening detainees with a loaded 9 mm pistol
- pouring cold water on naked detainees
- beating detainees with a broom handle and a chair
- threatening male detainees with rape
- allowing a military police guard to stitch the wound of a detainee who was injured after being slammed against the wall in his cell
- sodomizing a detainee with a chemical light and perhaps a broomstick
- using military working dogs (without muzzles) to frighten and intimidate detainees with threats of attack, and in at least one case biting and severely injuring a detainee
- forcing detainees to remove their clothing and keeping them naked for several days at a time
- forcing naked male detainees to wear women's underwear
- taking pictures of dead Iraqi detainees[8]

There is additional evidence that interrogation methods in violation of international human rights and humanitarian law were commonplace in Iraq. According to a transcript obtained by the *New York Times*, Colonel Thomas Pappas, commander of the 205th Military Intelligence Brigade, told General Taguba that intelligence officers sometimes instructed military police to strip detainees naked and to shackle them in preparation for interrogation when there was a "good reason" to do so. Lieutenant Colonel Jerry Phillabaum, the former top military police commander in Abu Ghraib, said in a written statement that military interrogators routinely used sleep deprivation and other forms of psychological intimidation to elicit information from prisoners. "The purpose of that wing of the prison was to isolate prisoners with intelligence, so that they would provide it during MI [military intelligence] interrogations," Phillabaum said.[9] The Reuters news agency reported that three of its Iraqi employees were detained near Fallujah in January 2004 and subjected to sleep deprivation with bags over their heads, forced to remain in stress positions for long periods, and beaten. A summary of the U.S. Army's 82nd Airborne Division's investigation provided to Reuters conceded that the detainees were "purposefully and carefully put under stress, to include sleep deprivation, in order to facilitate interrogation."[10]

CASES UNDER INVESTIGATION

From the earliest days of the U.S. occupation of Iraq, the U.S. government has been aware of allegations of abuses, including the death of some 30 persons in detention. Yet soldiers accused of abuse have—until after the Abu Ghraib scandal broke—escaped judicial punishment.[11] Several cases are still being investigated as possible homicides. To date, no one has been criminally charged in any of the cases.

Among the cases:

Camp Bucca

In one case dating from the first days of the occupation, three army reserve MPs (military police) allegedly beat prisoners and encouraged others to do so at Camp Bucca in the southern city of Um Qasr on May 12, 2003. The commanding officer at Camp Bucca was Lt. Colonel Phillabaum, later implicated in the Abu Ghraib abuses. Charges were brought against the military police but were ended with only their demotion and discharge. In his report, General Taguba noted that "following the abuse of several detainees at Camp Bucca in May 2003, I could find no evidence that BG [Brigadier General] Karpinski ever directed corrective training for her soldiers or ensured that MP soldiers throughout

Iraq clearly understood the requirements of the Geneva Conventions relating to the treatment of detainees."

Abed Hamed Mowhoush

Captured in October 2003, the former chief of Iraqi air defenses, Major General Abed Hamed Mowhoush, died November 26, 2003, at a detention facility at Al Qaim. The Pentagon first released a death certificate reporting that Mowhoush had died "of natural causes"; a news release added that "he did not feel well and subsequently lost consciousness." But following a report in the *Denver Post*[12] after the Abu Ghraib scandal erupted, the Pentagon acknowledged that according to an autopsy report, Mowhoush died of "asphyxia due to smothering and chest compression," showing "evidence of blunt force trauma to the chest and legs," and said that a homicide investigation was under way. Reportedly, Chief Warrant Officer Lewis Welshofer and another officer slid a sleeping bag over Mowhoush's head and rolled him over and over while asking questions. Welshofer is accused of sitting on Mowhoush's chest and placing his hands over his mouth. According to the investigative summary, "approximately 24 to 48 hours prior to (Mowhoush's death), Mowhoush was questioned by 'other governmental agency officials [i.e. the CIA],' and statements suggest that he was beaten during that interrogation."[13]

Karim 'Abd al-Jalil

A former lieutenant colonel in the Iraqi army, Kareem 'Abd al-Jalil died on January 9, 2004, at Forward Operating Base Rifles near al-Asad, where he was being interrogated by Special Forces since January 4. The original death certificate stated that he died of "natural causes . . . during his sleep." But pictures taken by 'Abd al-Jalil's cousin of his body before burial seem to depict severe bruises on his abdomen as well as marks and cuts on his arms and legs, especially around the wrists. Spiegel TV, a German news organization, interviewed another detainee held with 'Abd al-Jalil who stated that during interrogation, American soldiers "would kick him ['Abd al-Jalil] a lot, cuff his hands and place them behind his neck. And they would also cuff his feet, then one of them would hold his feet up while the other pulled down his head. They tossed him on his back and stepped on him. They danced on his belly and poured cold water all over him."[14] A Pentagon memo obtained by the *Denver Post* and reported by NBC says 'Abd al-Jalil was held in isolation, his hands tied to a pipe that ran along the ceiling. When he was untied, he attacked his interrogators and later tried to escape. When recaptured, his hands were tied to the top of his cell door and his mouth gagged.[15] Five minutes later, a guard noticed 'Abd al-Jalil dead, hanging by his shackles. After these revelations, the Pentagon released another certificate calling 'Abd al-Jalil's death a homicide from "blunt force injuries and asphyxia."[16] The Pentagon also said those who interrogated him included members of an elite Special Forces unit, some of the most highly trained personnel in the U.S. military.[17]

Nagm Sadoon Hatab

Former Baath Party official Nagm Sadoon Hatab was found dead at Camp Whitehorse detention facility near the southern Iraqi city of Nasiriyah on June 6, 2003.[18] The autopsy record said he died from "strangulation." Military records state that Hatab was asphyxiated when a marine guard grabbed his throat in an attempt to move him, accidentally breaking a bone that cut off his air supply. Another marine is charged with kicking Hatab in the chest in the hours before his death—several of his ribs were broken.[19] Hatab was also covered with feces and left under the sun for hours. The Marines believed Hatab had taken part in the ambush of Private First Class Jessica Lynch's unit and reportedly were instituting some form of vigilante justice. Eight marines were initially charged with various offenses related to Hatab's death; six later had the charges dropped or reduced to administrative punishment. The remaining two were tried. Major Clarke Paulus, who commanded Camp Whitehorse when Hatab died, was found guilty in November 2004 of maltreatment and dereliction of duty and was dismissed from the service. He was acquitted of more serious charges. Reservist Sergeant Gary Pittman, who was a guard at Whitehorse, was convicted of assaulting prisoners, was sentenced to 60 days' hard labor, and was reduced in rank to private. He received no jail time.[20]

REPORTS OF ABUSE IGNORED

Prior to the publication of the Abu Ghraib photos, the U.S. government had multiple opportunities to take all necessary action to address what officials should have recognized was a serious and widespread problem. In fact, the ICRC report states that it alerted U.S. authorities to abuses orally and in writing throughout 2003. In May 2003, the ICRC sent a memorandum based on over 200 allegations of ill-treatment of prisoners of war during capture and interrogation at collecting points, battle group stations, and temporary holding areas. That same month, the special representative of the United Nations secretary-general, Mr. Sergio Vieira de Mello, raised concerns about the treatment of detainees with the coalition administrator, Ambassador Paul Bremer.[21] In early July 2003, the ICRC presented a paper detailing approximately 50 allegations of ill-treatment in the military intelligence section of Camp Cropper, at Baghdad International Airport.

According to the ICRC these incidents included

a combination of petty and deliberate acts of violence aimed at securing the co-operation of the persons deprived of their liberty with their interrogators; threats (to intern individuals indefinitely, to arrest other family members,[22] to transfer individuals to Guantánamo) against persons deprived of their liberty or against members of their families (in particular wives and daughters); hooding; tight handcuffing; use of stress positions (kneeling, squatting, standing with arms raised over the head) for three or four hours; taking aim at individuals with rifles, striking them with rifle butts, slaps, punches, prolonged exposure to the sun, and isolation in dark cells. ICRC delegates witnessed marks on the bodies of several persons deprived of their liberty consistent with their allegations.

In one case, a detainee

alleged that he had been hooded and cuffed with flexi-cuffs, threatened to be tortured and killed, urinated on, kicked in the head, lower back and groin, force-fed a baseball which was tied into the mouth using a scarf and deprived of sleep for four consecutive days. Interrogators would allegedly take turns ill-treating him. When he said he would complain to the ICRC he was allegedly beaten more. An ICRC medical examination revealed hematoma in the lower back, blood in urine, sensory loss in the right hand due to tight handcuffing with flexi-cuffs, and a broken rib.

During a visit to Abu Ghraib prison in October 2003, ICRC delegates witnessed "the practice of keeping persons deprived of their liberty completely naked in totally empty concrete cells and in total darkness," the report said. "Upon witnessing such cases, the ICRC interrupted its visits and requested an explanation from the authorities. The military intelligence officer in charge of the interrogation explained that this practice was "part of the process."[23]

Rather than responding to these warning signals, however, according to one senior U.S. Army officer who served in Iraq, army officials responded to the report of abuses at Abu Ghraib prison by trying to curtail the ICRC's spot inspections, insisting that the ICRC should make appointments before visiting the cellblock.[24]

GUANTÁNAMO MEETS AFGHANISTAN AT ABU GHRAIB

In August 2003, Defense Secretary Rumsfeld, through his top intelligence aide, Stephen A. Cambone, sent Major General Geoffrey D. Miller, who oversaw the interrogation efforts at the U.S. military base at Guantánamo Bay, Cuba, to, in the words of Major General Taguba, "review current Iraqi Theater ability to rapidly exploit internees for actionable intelligence."[25] Miller was tasked in essence with "Gitmo-izing" interrogation practices in Iraq, although the Bush administration recognizes that the Geneva Conventions are "fully applicable" in Iraq[26] while it has said that they do not cover al Qaeda detainees at Guantánamo.[27]

As Taguba highlighted in his report, Miller recommended that "the guard force be actively engaged in setting the conditions for successful exploitation of the internees."[28] There is little clarity regarding what else Miller recommended.[29]

On October 12, Lieutenant General Ricardo Sanchez, then commanding general in Iraq, implemented Miller's proposals, issuing a classified memorandum calling for interrogators at Abu Ghraib to work with military police guards to "manipulate an internee's emotions and weaknesses" and to assume control over the "lighting, heating . . . food, clothing, and shelter" of those they were questioning.[30] The full contents of the Sanchez memo have not been made public.

In addition, between three and five interrogation teams were sent in October from Guantánamo to the American command in Iraq "for use in the interrogation effort" at Abu Ghraib.[31]

Capt. Carolyn A. Wood, who oversaw interrogations at the Bagram detention center in Afghanistan where two prisoners died, apparently prepared the document titled "Interrogation Rules of Engagement" that was posted at Abu Ghraib. According to the document, certain interrogation methods could be undertaken, but only if the "CG's" (Sanchez's) approval was sought and obtained in writing. Depending on their actual application, these methods would violate the Geneva Conventions' prohibitions against abusive and coercive treatment of detainees. They included:

- Change of scenery down (moving to a more barren cell)
- Dietary manipulation
- Environmental manipulation
- Sleep adjustment (reverse schedule)
- Isolation for longer than 30 days
- Presence of military working dogs
- Sleep management (72 hours maximum)
- Sensory deprivation (72 hours maximum)
- Stress positions (no longer than 45 minutes)

The document also cautions that detainees "will NEVER be touched in a malicious or unwanted manner" and that the Geneva Conventions apply in Iraq.

Even though his title appears on the document, which also carried the logo of Combined Joint Task Force-7, the U.S.-led coalition force in Iraq, General Sanchez denies having seen or approved the rules of engagement posted at Abu Ghraib (although he acknowledged that in twenty-five separate instances, he approved holding Iraqi prisoners in isolation for longer than thirty days, one of the methods listed in the posted rules). Keith B. Alexander, the head of the Army intelligence, however, said that they were the approved policy for interrogations of detainees in Iraq.[32]

What is clear is that U.S. military personnel at Abu Ghraib felt empowered to abuse the detainees. The brazenness with which the soldiers at the center of the scandal conducted themselves, snapping photographs and flashing the "thumbs-up" sign as they abused prisoners, suggests they felt they had nothing to hide from their superiors. The abuse was so widely known and accepted that a picture of naked detainees forced into a human pyramid was reportedly used as a screen saver on a computer in the interrogation room.[33] According to Major General Taguba, "interrogators actively requested that MP guards set physical and mental conditions for favorable interrogation of witnesses.... [The] MP Brigade [was] directed to change facility procedures to 'set the conditions' for military intelligence interrogations." Taguba cited the testimony of several military police: "One said the orders were 'Loosen this guy up for us. Make sure he has a bad night. Make sure he gets the treatment.'" Another stated that "the prison wing belongs to [Military Intelligence] and it appeared that MI personnel approved the abuse." That MP also noted that "[t]he MI staffs, to my understanding, have been giving Graner [an MP in charge of night shifts at Abu Ghraib] compliments on the way he has been handling the MI [detainees]. Example being statements like 'Good job, they're breaking down real fast.'"

General Sanchez announced on May 14, 2004, that he had barred the use of coercive interrogation techniques including "stress positions," "sleep deprivation," and the use of hoods, that had previously been available, though it is still not clear what he had previously approved.

NOTES

1   Convention against Torture and Other Cruel, Inhuman, Degrading Treatment or Punishment

2   *See* Letter on HRW's Concerns About the Rights of Iraqi Detainees, February 10, 2004, http://hrw.org/english/docs/2004/02/10/iraq8471.htm.

3   Douglas Jehl and Kate Zernike, "Scant Evidence Cited in Long Detention of Iraqis," *New York Times,* May 30, 2004.

4 "Report of the International Committee of the Red Cross (ICRC) on the Treatment by the Coalition Forces of Prisoners of War and Other Protected Persons by the Geneva Conventions in Iraq During Arrest, Internment and Interrogation," February 2004 (hereafter "ICRC report").

5 As Major General Antonio Taguba noted in his report, recent intelligence collection in support of Operation Enduring Freedom (the war in Afghanistan) posited a template whereby military police actively set favorable conditions for subsequent interviews. Investigative report on alleged abuses at U.S. military prisons in Abu Ghraib and Camp Bucca, Iraq, by Maj. Gen. Antonio M. Taguba: "Article 15-6 Investigation of the 800th Military Police Brigade" (hereafter "Taguba report").

6 Matt Kelley, "Military Intelligence Troops Accused of Abuses in Four Camps Outside Abu Ghraib," May 29, 2004.

7 Interestingly, this was not referred to as rape, although the threat to forcibly have sex with male detainees was referred to as rape.

8 Taguba report.

9 Sewell Chan and Thomas E. Ricks, "Iraq Prison Supervisors Face Army Reprimand," *Washington Post*, May 4, 2004.

10 Andrew Marshall, "Reuters Staff Abused by U.S. in Iraq," Reuters, May 18, 2004.

11 Under the U.S. Uniform Code of Military Justice, military personnel may be subject to so-called nonjudicial punishment via an article 15 administrative hearing or to prosecution by court-martial. Article 15 punishments include up to one-year imprisonment, fines, loss of rank, and discharge from the military.

12 Arthur Kane and Miles Moffeit, "Carson GI Eyed in Jail Death Iraqi General Died in Custody," *Denver Post*, May 28, 2004.

13 Robert Weller, "Soldier Investigated in Iraqi General's Death: Officer at Fort Carson Says There Is an 'Agenda,'" Associated Press, May 29, 2004.

14 Chris Hansen, "Profile: Death in Custody."

15 "The Homicide Cases," editorial, *Washington Post*, May 28, 2004.

16 Chris Hansen, "Profile: Death in Custody."

17 Chris Hansen, "Profile: Death in Custody."

18 Tom Squitieri and Dave Moniz, "3rd of Detainees Who Died Were Assaulted; Shot, Strangled, Beaten, Certificates Show," *USA Today*, June 1, 2004.

19 "Did Abuses Go Beyond Abu Ghraib?" CBS News, May 29, 2004.

20 Alex Roth and Jeff McDonald, "Iraqi Detainee's Death Hangs over Marine Unit," *San Diego Union-Tribune,* May 30, 2004; and Rick Rogers, "Abuse Charges Against Marine Reservist Are Dismissed," *San Diego Union-Tribune,* April 13, 2004.

21 *See Report of the Secretary-General to the U.N. Security Council*, July 17, 2003, S/2003/715, para. 47.

22 In November 2003, coalition forces arrested the wife and daughter of General Izzat Ibrahim al-Douri, former vice-chair of Iraq's Revolutionary Command Council and a top Saddam Hussein associate, apparently as hostages, in violation of the Geneva Conventions. *See* Human Rights Watch letter to Defense Secretary Donald Rumsfeld, January 12, 2004. Available at: http://www.hrw.org/english/docs/2004/01/12/usint6921_txt.htm.

23 "Red Cross: Iraq Abuse 'Tantamount to Torture': Agency Says U.S. Was Repeatedly Given Details of Mistreatment," MSNBC News, May 11, 2004.

24 Douglas Jehl and Eric Schmitt, "Army Tried to Limit Abu Ghraib Access," *New York Times*, May 20, 2004. The article also quotes Brigadier General Janis Karpinski, commander of the 800th Military Police Brigade, whose soldiers guarded the prisoners, as saying that senior officers in Baghdad had treated the ICRC report in "a light-hearted manner."

25 Taguba later decried Miller's idea of transporting interrogation techniques from Guantánamo to Iraq, noting that there were major differences between the status of the detainees in the two locations.

26 Douglas Jehl and Neil A. Lewis, "U.S. disputed protected status of Iraq inmates," *New York Times*, May 23, 2004. *See also*, Alberto R. Gonzales, "The Rule of Law and the Rules of War," *New York Times*, May 15, 2004 ("Both the United States and Iraq are parties to the Geneva Conventions. The United States recognizes that these treaties are binding in the war for the liberation of Iraq. There has never been any suggestion by our government that the conventions do not apply in that conflict.")

27 Miller testified that "no program" at Guantánamo "has any of those techniques that are prohibited by the Geneva Convention." But Sanchez, said that the procedures Miller brought from Guantánamo to Iraq "have to be modified" because "the Geneva Convention was fully applicable" in Iraq, in contrast to Guantánamo. Editorial, "Reveal the Rules," *Washington Post*, May 23, 2004.

28 Taguba took issue with this proposal and noted that it would be "in conflict with" the recommendations of the Ryder Report, a previous review of Iraqi prisons which stated that the engagement of military police in military interrogations to "actively set the favorable conditions for subsequent interviews runs counter to the smooth operation of a detention facility."

29 According to Thomas Pappas, the U.S. army officer in charge of the prison cells at Abu Ghraib, one of Miller's recommendations was the use of military guard dogs in interrogations. Pappas also stated that the recommendation was approved by Lt. Gen. Ricardo S. Sanchez, the top U.S. military official in Iraq. Both Miller and Sanchez deny this. R. Jeffrey Smith, "General is Said to Have Urged Used of Dogs," *Washington Post*, May 26, 2004; Scott Higham, Joe Stephens and Josh White, "Prison Visits by General Reported in Hearing; Alleged Presence of Sanchez Cited by Lawyer," *Washington Post*, May 23, 2004.

30 *See* R. Jeffrey Smith, "Memo gave intelligence bigger role: increased pressure sought on prisoners," *Washington Post*, May 21, 2004.

31 Douglas Jehl and Andrea Elliott, "Cuba base sent its interrogators to Iraqi prison, New York Times, May 29, 2004.

32 Editorial, "Reveal the rules," *Washington Post*, May 23, 2004.

33 Kate Zernike, "Only a few spoke up on abuse as many soldiers stayed silent," *New York Times,* May 22, 2004.

6
Statement

Kenneth Scott

Kenneth Scott was born in Jamaica and moved to the United States in 1985. He was picked up by the INS on October 29, 2001, after serving a criminal sentence for a drug-related offense. Kenneth has spent the last three years in jail, fighting his deportation.

MY NAME IS KENNETH SCOTT. I was picked up and detained by the INS after I was released from prison on October 29, 2001. I was brought to the Hudson County Jail in New Jersey.

While I was being held they take me to see an Immigration Judge. I was shackled from 7:30 am till 4:30 pm. Everybody had to stay shackled up all day, except when they bring you lunch, they loosen one hand so you can eat.

After going to court for three months the Judge order me deported and they sent me to Middlesex County Jail, N.J. While I was there the detainees went through hell with the officers because the INS told them that we were terrorist from New York City and that we were very dangerous. So they beat us up. Every morning was a cell search and someone end up getting beat up by the officers. After awhile enough was enough and we start fighting back by going on hunger strike.

After 9 months in that jail, they move me to Passaic County Jail. Oh boy if that jail wasn't hell I don't know. No one can tell me that was not hell. The officers at that jail were the most racist Police I ever met. They call you names. When they have shackle you down they throw your property all over the place including your legal work and if you say anything they beat you up like there is no tomorrow and they come with dogs and if the dogs bark at you, they say it is your fault, and beat you more.

I have been detain for 20 months now without any outside help. You just have to sit in here on rotting. Your family and friends give up on you. After a while most of them don't know what to do or what is going on because the INS won't tell them anything about you.

7

Looking for Hope: Life as an Immigration Detainee

Phillip Marcus

Phillip Marcus was born in Guyana and moved to the United States in 1968. He became a lawful permanent resident in 1976 and raised four children in Brooklyn. Like Kenneth Scott, Phillip was taken into INS custody after serving a sentence for a drug-related crime. He spent over a year in immigration detention before being deported to Guyana.

DAY 1

I was arrested by the INS at 10:00 am on July 12, 2002, and taken to Varick Street [New York City] for processing. While I was there, they brought in three other detainees. After we were processed we were handcuffed and chained with leg irons and transferred to Middlesex Correctional Center at 9:00 pm. At Middlesex we were processed, strip-searched, and sent to "N pod" to sleep at about 1:00 am.

DAY 2

I was awoken by a cellmate who'd been asleep when I came in, and he told me it was time for breakfast. At breakfast I discovered that there were other detainees housed in this unit and that we all wear red jumpsuits. I also found out that we were housed together with regular county prisoners, some who'd committed violent crimes. While eating I met three other detainees like myself, one from Barbados, one from Trinidad, and one from Jamaica. I quickly found out what we all had in common other than being immigration detainees. I found out that we were all unsure of our fates and were looking for any hope.

Later that day the officer in charge of N pod started calling names out. I quickly inquired why he was calling out these people's names, and was told they were going to other units in the jail, and when they have enough immigration detainees they will soon be moving us out of N pod.

DAY 3

When you are locked up, every day seems to be the same: you eat at the same time, lock down at the same time, and so on. The only difference for me this day was that they called my name: 48 of us were moved to A pod. The entire unit was empty, and everybody got to choose who they wanted to cell with.

EVERY OTHER DAY

Every other day seems the same, the same routine, the same food, the same bars on our cells. We all wanted to know when we were going to court. The jail has a staff of social workers that is supposed to come around and take information, and help with phone calls so we can contact our families. The bad luck we had was to draw the worst social worker in the jail. This guy would come in with an attitude, go into a room, close the door, and not see or speak to anybody all day.

One day a detainee from Jordan came to the pod. I will admit this guy was very aggressive—he doesn't take "no" too lightly. The social worker came in as usual, went into his room and locked the door: the new guy went and knocked on the door, and the social worker came out and started cursing at him. An argument ensued, and the social worker punched the Jordanian guy in his face. A fight started, the officer on duty called for help, and the other officers came and hit the detainee with pepper spray. The sergeant then locked all of us in our cells for three days. I later found out that this social worker filled out a questionnaire about me without ever having spoken to me.

JULY 31, MOVING DAY

After we ate breakfast an officer informed seven of us that we must pack up all of our property because we are leaving the facility. About 40 of us were transferred to Passaic County Jail in Paterson, New Jersey. When I left Middlesex I bought about $40 worth of items at the commissary, but when I got to Passaic the intake officer threw most of it in the trash, saying they don't sell potato chips and whatnot in this jail. We were moved from holding cell to holding cell for six hours before we were issued a mattress, one dirty sheet, and a towel. We were sent to the fourth floor, where they already had other INS detainees housed, and squirreled into 4G3 dorm, which has 60 beds—double and triple bunks—three showers with only two working, one urinal and three toilets for 56 detainees. There were no windows and no air-conditioning, and the air vent was covered in mildew, as were the walls.

We quickly found out that the officers here at Passaic County Jail would beat us and use dogs to threaten us. Whenever we were going to recreation, they pushed our faces up against the wall; in fact they did this anytime we left the unit. We also found out that when you complain about receiving the same type of food for two days, such as peanut butter, the only answer is that the kitchen is not controlled by the jail and there is nothing they can do about it. Sometimes as a punishment the officers would come into the dorm and give it a shakedown by throwing all of our property on the floor—our clothes, anything we had from the commissary, and all our legal papers. Sometimes they would even throw our property away. When they come to shake down they come into the dorm with about twenty officers, the K-9 dogs, and an officer with a gun: this happens three or four times a week. It is also customary for the shakedowns to take place at one and two o'clock in the morning.

THE INS AND GOING TO COURT

When somebody went to court, we'd all sit around waiting to find out what had happened. We wanted to know the name of the judge, whether he is lenient to detainees, or anything and everything that could give us hope. After a while, we realized that less than 10 percent of us would be allowed out on bond and that out of the 90 percent of us left, 89 percent of us will be ordered removed from the United States. The final thing we all came to accept is that those who appeal their case will spend over a year fighting or waiting, with no relief. The thing that surprised me is that people, including myself, were willing to hold on to that slim ray of hope, hoping for something to change or break.

MY LIFE AND WHY I CHOSE TO FIGHT

I cannot claim to be the world's number one father, but I can tell you of my love for my children. I have four children, Jerome (21), Asia (18), who is about to enter the University of Georgia, Phillip Jr. (16), and Tamara (13). As any parent would say, their children are their life, and it's no different with me. I would love to be there for my children. I want hug them when they need that hug. I want guide them when they need guidance. And most of all, I want them to know that I am there when they need me to be there. I have lived my whole life in Brooklyn. I attended P.S. 183, Junior High 275, and South Shore High School. I joined the United States Army in 1983 and was discharged in 1987. I have worked at many Fortune 500 companies such as AIG Insurance and AT&T

Wireless. I have two felonies, one for importation of cocaine, and the other for wire fraud. I served two terms in federal prison, 41 months and 48 months. When I first came to the INS and the immigration judge ordered me deported, I told my family that I was tired of being locked up and it was time for me to leave. They said I should try to fight and when I give up it should be because I have no more recourse. I have been married for 18 years, and I think this life in limbo has finally taken its toll on my marriage. So, now I am sitting waiting for the immigration judge to reopen my INS case for one last shot at freedom in the United States.

8

Statement

Hemnauth Mohabir

Hemnauth Mohabir is a musician, born in Guyana. He lived in the United States, had a green card, and was married to an American citizen. In 1997, he pled guilty to a drug misdemeanor, to avoid facing jail time, and paid a $250 fine. Five years later, he was picked up by immigration while reentering the country after visiting his ailing mother in Guyana. He spent a year and a half in immigration detention, fighting his deportation and organizing the other detainees, before being deported to Guyana.

GREETINGS TO ALL the peacemakers, for you are surely God's children. My name is Hemnauth Mohabir. I was born in Georgetown, Guyana. I've always been a musician by profession. I served my country for two years in the early eighties as a cultural coordinator and musician in the department of culture.

I met my wife in the mid-eighties. She was a dancer, and I was a guitar player in a band while doing a coast-to-coast tour of Guyana and Suriname. In 1988 we were given the golden opportunity to live and take care of the pandit's council, the largest Hindu temple in Guyana, by the Minister of Labor, who was a Hindu priest and a friend. My wife and I enjoyed serving the community in this special way.

My wife migrated to the U.S. in the late '80s while I toured the West Indies and filed a petition for me to join her in the USA. After my contract expired in '93 I joined her. My band got a new contract to Europe and Asia, which I turned down because my one and only son, Rajendra, was now creeping around. I decided to enroll at Apex Technical School, to seek a better life for my family, and to pursue my dream of recording the songs I've been writing since I was in high school, based on our struggle as Guyanese people.

In '96 a friend and I were entrapped by the police to look like drug dealers. We went to trial, and because we were innocent the judge dismissed two felony charges. My lawyer said it would be best to accept a misdemeanor charge. A dollar bill was found on the ground with cocaine the quantity of half a grain of rice in size, the dollar bill was marked money because it belonged to the undercover police. The police refused to show us the print of the marked money. The trial ended in September of '97. At the sentencing my lawyer stayed with me to see if the charge of possession of a controlled substance in the seventh degree would affect my resident status. The sentence was to pay a fine of $250 and have my driver's license suspended for six months. My lawyer said that it did not affect my green card and that everything was OK.

One day I got a call that my mother, who I hadn't seen in nine years, was very sick in Guyana. So I left for Guyana on the sixth of April, 2002. After spending two weeks with my mom I came back to the USA on the twentieth of April, 2002, and was told at JFK Airport that the misdemeanor charge from 1997 violated my resident status. I was then arrested and chained at the feet and hands. They held me at the airport for 24 hours. After I made arrangements for Rahoni to collect my suitcases, the INS came and walked me through the airport, I felt so humiliated, as if I was torn to pieces, as all eyes was on me, as I looked at the people, I can hear them saying to themselves. Maybe he is a terrorist, or maybe he tried to enter illegally, or maybe he had illegal substance on him. The kind of life I've lived is to prevent things like this. I've traveled a bit, and I always make sure my papers are right, and I do not have any sharp-edged stuff on me or illegal substances and I don't go around hurting people or any living thing.

I was taken to Middlesex County Correctional Center. My blood pressure was high, for this was the first time that I've seen what jail looks like. They had me walking with handcuffs in the building while going to the doctor to check my blood pressure every day, even the regular inmates who saw me handcuffed in a maximum-security jail, looked on with surprise. This lasted for three days, before they moved me to the "H" pod, a large dorm.

As an arriving alien I was not entitled to bond, and although I have a green card, I was treated as if I tried to enter the country illegally. I can assure you that was never my intention. The INS claims that because the charge occurred in '97 and I came in '93 which is four years difference, I violated my resident status, and I was not entitled to any form of relief.

In August, four months after I was detained, I finally got my hearing. The judge stopped the tape and said, "Mr Mohabir, you are an extremely honest man." He then turned to my lawyer and said, "this is a stupid charge, a stupid case, and I have to make a stupid decision on this man to get him out of detention, either vacate the charge or file parole," and that he'll give us two months to do so, and when he makes a decision we can appeal. My lawyer showed up at Middlesex Correctional Center and said that he works for two hundred dollars an hour, and that the money has finished, but he'll see me through this. I was ordered removed from the USA on the twenty-fifth of September, I learned this from an INS officer. Mr. Allen then filed to reopen the case to the BIA and sent the bill to Rahoni, we never heard from him since.

In October the INS moved me to the Passaic County Jail, which is a torture chamber. I cannot believe that such a jail exist like this in the USA who boast of its freedoms and civil rights.

The building is very old and it has a lot of cracks in the roof, which leaks all the time and makes the dorm smell like dirty socks. The dorm has this big exhaust fan and the damper is broken which causes cold air and water to fall through it easily. In November of 2002 when winter kicked in, they used the fan to blow the outside air inside and freeze us up. We all stayed in bed for roll call and breakfast, because it was too cold. The captain came and we explain our problem, then they moved us to some cells where it was a lit-tle warmer, there I shared a cell with Farouk Abdel Muhti who I had known from Middlesex. The INS doesn't want to release him because he is an activist from Palestine and a spokesperson for WBAI Radio so we started writing together and making contact with various human rights organizations.

The food was still cold, the food is very small in portion, and the vegetarians would get beans out of the can into the trays, peanut butter and macaroni, or two slices of cheese with a spoon of rice. The jail is roach infested, the bathroom is sometimes very cold and sometimes very hot and sometimes it goes from 160° F to 60° F in a very short time, I got sick from the hot and cold water.

The police does these shakedowns on a regular basis. They would come in the dorm with a dog and put all of us against the bars and search the dorm. They would throw all of our legal paperwork, mattress, and commissary all over mixing them up. Imagine a police stamping his feet on a metal table, a dog bark-ing and jumping, and the police yelling, "Put your F—— face at the bar," and they would be running around like they gone crazy. One day a detainee was in the bathroom during a shakedown, an officer pulled him out and beat him, two more police joined him, and I saw the detainee's head bleeding.

In January 2003 about twenty of us went on a hunger strike. Eight of us wanted to be transferred to Hudson County Jail, the rest of us wanted them to better the food at least cook it and give it a little taste, and for them to be cautious with their shake downs. Things did improve, we now got salt on the trays, so the food can have taste. The other guys got transferred to Hudson County. Brother Farouk was transferred to York County Jail and was placed in solitary confinement. After two weeks things got sloppy again.

In March the police placed among us a detainee who works as an informer. We were well organized. The detainee wrote a note to the captain and identified eight of us. The police came in the dorm with their dog and began to shake down. The eight of us had to pack up while the rest had to face the bars. Between the dog and the bunks there is a ten-feet space, where we have to pass with our bags and mattress. Another detainee was in front of me, the dog jumped at him. He pulled away from the dog, a police then ran up to him and hit him on his head and pushed him into the ground by his face, the rest of the police started running around like crazy, one came up to my face, and push his finger in my face, and yell in my face "You want to say something," "Do you have anything to say." In the meantime two more officers jumped on the other detainee, and was trying to hand cuff him, it was very difficult, because too many hands was on him, they started hitting him in his ribs, he started yelling, "Look my hands put the cuff on." Imagine one police knees in his back and his hand pushing the detainee's head into the floor while the other two fumbled with his hand. After this they took us down in a bull pen. We decided to go on a hunger strike, protesting the police brutality, and to be transferred to another jail. During the night of the second day the police came to do roll call with a dog. One senior officer started cursing me because I was moving a bit slow because I was on a top bunk and was being careful climbing off. He said "get the F—— off your bed you F—— asshole," I was caught by surprise, I replied by saying "Shut up it don't call for that." He said "what, open this gate." He, a dog, and a sergeant came in and put us against the wall. A lieutenant slammed his hands on my ribs, I pant for breath, he kept rubbing his hands up and down my side, I turned and said "Please don't hit me," he said "You are all right," he then hit me harder in the ribs, I felt my breath cut for a minute. When we turned around after they moved out the bull pen, they had thrown a mattress on the floor. They threw all the mattress on the floor, scattered all of our legal paperwork all over the floor, they flushed our towels and sheets in the toilet bowl, they tore up a bible. I could feel the wind moving behind me, as the dog was moving close behind me, the police who had the dog grab at my hair to take off a string which I used to tie it. I saw another officer pushing his finger in another detainee's face, and grabbing another one by the hair, they then went out laughing.

I saw another detainee beaten. They spit in his face. He suffered injuries in the ribs and head. One morning we had problems with the food and an officer said "you F—— immigrants" and made sexual remarks insulting us.

I remember in August we were downstairs at the court at 970 Broad Street, and a man from Italy was being deported. He was not so good at speaking English, he asked the officers if he can change his cheak [cheque] they didn't answer him. He then said that he had a right to change his cheque. A male officer ran up to him and threw him on the ground by his face, the man was chained at his feet and a handcuff on his hand stuck to a chain around his waist, so his movements were restricted. The officer put his knees in the man's back and was tugging his head, his other hand on his gun. The man was screaming. I couldn't bare it so I said "You have no right to do that." The officer told the other officer to take us inside and while we were going inside I saw the officer pick up the man and throw him on a car trunk by his back and start smacking him in his face. The man was charged for assaulting the officer and had to spend three more months in jail before being deported.

I am trying to fight my deportation because I want to be there for my son. It is my duty to take care of him. It's a hurt I'll have to live with for the rest of my life that I did not do my duty as a father if I have to leave him. My son wrote a letter saying how he used to enjoy the little walks and talks we used to have, and the research we used to do in the library, he even sent a certificate of excellence, which he got for his science project, and he said that he really missed me and wants me to come home. His mother sent me a letter saying that she cannot pay the phone bill for the collect calls I make from the jail, so she had to restrict her phone from collect calls, and she had to give up the apartment in Queens and settle for a studio apartment in the Bronx. She is very worried about what will happen to her and my son, when I'm gone.

I've completed tracks for my album which just needs to be mixed. It hard to accept that the dreams I had since I was a young child, to spread God's message in the form of music and to have a wonderful family, was becoming visible, and it just suddenly disappeared and is replaced with pain, suffering and stress. I still have my sanity, so everything in my head is still there, the rest is just material things. Maybe it's God's way of purging one's heart and mind. In a situation like this, where one is detached from material things, one gets a sense that there is a greater purpose in life that we have no control over, so we just have to learn to accept the things that we cannot change, while we strive to change the things we can. For God doesn't give you more than you can bare.

God bless you all. Peace to the world.
Hemnauth Mohabir
June 4, 2003

9

The Post-9/11 Terrorism Investigation and Immigration Detention

Rachel Meeropol

ON ANY GIVEN DAY, over 20,000 men, women, and children languish in indefinite detention in the United States.[1] These individuals are not in jail awaiting trial on criminal charges or serving a sentence for a past crime; nor have they been subject to civil commitment based on mental illness. Rather, these thousands of people are "immigration detainees," and they comprise the fastest-growing population of incarcerated people in the country with the highest incarceration rate in the world. Immigration detainees serve indeterminate sentences in federally run detention facilities, state prisons and county jails, as well as private facilities licensed by the federal government, under conditions that are often deplorable and inhuman. The length and conditions of their detention are insulated from review in most cases, because unlike pretrial detainees, those who cannot afford to hire an attorney are not provided with one free of charge. Those who are lucky enough to have access to an attorney find that their own or their counsel's efforts to shed light on poor conditions frequently result in the detainee's transfer to far-flung facilities. Buttressed by draconian legislation and anti-immigrant discrimination, the U.S. system of immigration detention has become a tool of repression wielded at the will of the executive and sheltered from meaningful scrutiny by the judiciary.

Our immigration policy is troubling enough in itself; even more troubling, however, is its proven and potential use as a tool to control and subjugate marginalized segments of society. While the government's excessive and unlawful actions in the wake of September 11, 2001 form the focus of this inquiry, it is equally important to understand how our immigration laws facilitate this level of oppression, and how our law is wielded, in combination with racial and ethnic profiling, to the detriment of our security and justice concerns. In this chapter, we will explore the details of the post-9/11 detentions, the conditions and duration of this form of detention, legal challenges to the detentions, and the policy and security implications of fighting terrorism through racial profiling and pretextual use of the immigration law.

ROUNDING UP THE "TERRORIST" NEXT DOOR

Immediately following the September 11 attacks, rumors spread through Brooklyn and across the country that men from (or appearing to be from) Arab, Muslim, and South Asian countries had disappeared from their homes and jobs. The disappearances were cloaked in secrecy. Wives, friends, parents, and siblings made frantic calls first to the police and immigration officers, and then to lawyers and reporters, but they were unable to find out any information about their loved ones' whereabouts. For much of the following year, immigrant rights groups and civil liberties watchdog organizations struggled to gain access to information on exactly where these men had been taken, and under what authority they were being held. While community activists and organizers were able to piece together a frightening story of racial profiling, illegal arrest, prolonged harsh detention, and physical and mental abuse, it was not until the Office of the Inspector General published a report on the detentions in April of 2003 (OIG report) that a detailed account of the government's actions became available. The following information is taken from that report, as well as from interviews by lawyers at the Center for Constitutional Rights conducted in preparation for their class-action challenge to the detentions, *Turkmen v. Ashcroft*, discussed later in this chapter.

After the attacks, the FBI, as part of the Pentagon/Twin Towers Bombings investigation (PENTTBOM) began preparing a watch list of individuals potentially connected to the terrorist acts, or who might have information about future attacks.[2] This list originally included individuals whose names were somehow linked to the hijackers. In that first week, Attorney General John Ashcroft transmitted a memo to all U.S. Attorneys instructing them to arrest and detain individuals connected to terrorism through "every available law enforcement tool."[3] The importance of immigration detention in this tool kit was immediately apparent. In a speech on October 25, 2001, Ashcroft exclaimed: "Let the terrorists among us be warned: If you overstay your visa—even by one day—we will arrest you. . . . We will use every available statute. We will seek every prosecutorial advantage."[4] Justice Department officials understood this mandate to require law enforcement to hold—by any means necessary—individuals suspected of having any link to terrorism, be it tenuous or totally unsupported, even if it meant enforcing immigration laws in a much stricter manner than is typical.[5]

With these instructions, the roundups began. FBI officers, charged with following up on thousands of tips pouring in across the country, began to investigate individuals, mostly noncitizens of color, for any possible connection to terrorist activity. The avalanche of tips flowing in, and the officers' own investigative stops, were largely based on racial profiling, and the vast majority lacked any evidence connecting the targets to terrorism. "Concerned citizens" called in to report Arab neighbors who kept "strange hours," and officers making routine traffic stops scrutinized the appearance of drivers and passengers.[6]

Despite scanty reason for suspicion, many of the subjects of these discriminatory tips and stops became targets of the PENTTBOM investigation. If, at the end of an investigative interview, the FBI or INS officer on the scene had reason to believe that the suspect was in violation of the immigration code—even without any evidence or suggestion of terrorist activity—that individual was arrested and held in connection to the terrorism investigation. In many cases, after beginning the information-gathering process, the investigating officer would also dispatch an INS officer to determine the immigration status of any person he or she simply happened to encounter while following leads. Anyone who could be arrested due to any violation of the immigration law was vulnerable to this dragnet, and in this way, hundreds of noncitizens with no connection to any criminal activity, let alone terrorism, were arrested and held as "post-9/11 detainees."

For example, the OIG report includes the story of a man arrested on immigration charges after he was found with a roll of film including pictures of the World Trade Center. This man, *and his roommates*, who were undocumented, were all arrested and classified as "of interest" to the terrorism investigation.[7] In another example, NYPD officers stopped three Middle Eastern men for a traffic violation and found plans for a public school in their car. Although their employer verified their positions the next day and explained that the men had the plans for a legitimate construction project at the school, the men were still arrested and detained as "of interest" to the terrorism investigation.[8] While there was some variation across the country, in New York individuals were arrested and labeled "of interest" without any attempt to distinguish the subject of a tip or lead from individuals randomly encountered while following that lead, or any attempt to examine the quality of the information leading to the arrest.[9]

To avoid "mistakenly releasing a potential terrorist," individuals for whom there was absolutely no evidence to suggest terrorist activities were arrested and subjected to a series of arbitrary, cruel, and unnecessary polices, described below. According to the OIG report, 762 noncitizens were arrested in these initial sweeps. Of course, verifying these numbers is impossible given the secrecy with which the detentions and the related deportations were conducted, and civil liberties activists and grassroots organizers place the number at closer to two thousand.

CONDITIONS OF DETENTION

Upon arrest, post-9/11 detainees were split into three categories based on the arresting FBI officer's assessment of whether the individual was of "high interest," "interest," or "interest undetermined" to the terrorism investigation.[10] Theoretically, "high interest" detainees included those with the highest potential for having a link to terrorism and "of interest" detainees "might" have such a link.[11] However, this determination was not based on any specific criteria, nor was it applied uniformly. Even more problematic, "interest undetermined" detainees included all those individuals who had somehow been swept up in the investigation, for whom the FBI could not marshal any evidence leading to any terrorism connection. Under orders of the Justice Department, detainees in all three of these categories were to be held until the FBI could disprove any potential connection to the 9/11 attacks.[12]

The FBI turned over its interest assessment to what was then INS, who made housing determinations accordingly. This had the greatest impact on the "high interest" detainees, who were sent to Metropolitan Detention Center (MDC), a federal facility in Brooklyn, New York. Bureau of Prisons (BOP) officials and the officers at MDC considered the "high interest" detainees to be extremely dangerous despite (or without knowledge of) the fact that this classification was arbitrary and meaningless. Thus, individuals without any criminal history, charged with civil violations, were subjected to conditions reserved for the most dangerous of the most dangerous.

The post-9/11 detainees were placed in the administrative maximum special housing unit (ADMAX SHU) at MDC. To understand the significance of the post-9/11 detainees' placement there, it is important to understand a bit about special housing units in general. Special housing units are supermaximum (or "supermax") security wings in lower-security facilities. Supermax prisons, on the other hand, are institutions entirely devoted to extreme restriction. The conditions of each are very similar. In the past decade and a half there has been a proliferation of new, supermaximum-security prisons. Upwards of 42 states now have supermax facilities. About one-third of these facilities have been opened in the last five years, and one-half in the last ten years. These extremely restrictive prisons are the modern equivalent of the "hole"—instead of torturing prisoners with solitary confinement in dark and dirty underground cells, prisoners are now subjected to solitary confinement in well-lit, sterile boxes. The psychological impact is similar.

These new prisons, or prison wings, are designed to minimize contact between inmates and staff, as well as to minimize contact among inmates themselves. Once inside, prisoners are subjected to extreme social isolation and sensory deprivation. Some prisoners serve out entire sentences—decades—in these conditions. The typical supermax cell is windowless and has a solid door. Most are smaller than 80 square feet. Prisoners are sealed into their cell for twenty-three to twenty-four hours a day. Recreation involves being taken, often in handcuffs and shackles, to another solitary cell, maybe with an open front, so as to be considered "outside" recreation. The cells have a toilet and a shower, and a slot in the door large enough for a guard to slip through a food tray. The cells are lit twenty-four hours a day and are often kept just cool enough to make sleep difficult. Most of these institutions do not have any work or education programs, although some offer programming via television.

Studies have shown that prolonged stays in solitary confinement cause physical and psychological damage. One court-appointed expert inspecting a supermax facility in Texas described an environment in which "smeared feces, self-mutilation, and incessant babbling and shrieking" were everyday occurrences. Often it is hard to divide cause and effect. Prisoners with mental illnesses typically receive terribly inadequate treatment, and their unchecked symptoms are frequently viewed by correctional officers as simple "behavior problems." For this reason many individuals with mental illnesses end up in ultrarestrictive confinement.

While proponents insist that the SHU and supermax facilities are necessary to control the worst of the worst, the numbers just don't add up. One Heritage report noted that "the 288 most dangerous convicts in Maryland are incarcerated in 'supermax,'" Maryland's Correctional Adjustment Center.[13] The reporter noted, a page later, that 105 murderers and 19 rapists spend their days in restrictive confinement in Supermax, raising the question: Who are the other 164 inmates?[14]

According to a 2000 Amnesty International Report, more than 20,000 prisoners are currently being held in long-term isolation in supermax facilities across the country.[15] Criteria for placement in supermax prisons and SHUs varies by state, but they uniformly place great weight on the discretionary judgments of prison administrators as to future dangerousness. Often, after spending significant tax dollars to construct these new prisons, administrators are hard-pressed to fill them—and end up placing prisoners inside who nobody believes deserve to be there.

Ever since solitary confinement has existed, it has been used as a tool of repression. While it is justified as necessary to protect inmates and guards from violent superpredators, all too often it is imposed on individuals who threaten prison administrations in an altogether different way. Consistently, jailhouse lawyers and jailhouse doctors who administer to the needs of their fellow inmates behind bars are placed in solitary confinement. They are joined by political prisoners from various civil rights and independence movements. In his book *Lockdown America* Christian Parenti documented the use of San Quentin's administrative segregation in the 1960s to punish militant prisoners and other incorrigibles: writers, artists, poets, communists, nationalists, and POWs.[16] Back in the day, solitary confinement teemed with radical books smuggled from cell to cell and covert study sessions. Today, of course, with the advent of super high-tech supermaximum-security prisons, study circles are a thing of the past, but the population remains the same.

In light of this history, placement of the post-9/11 detainees in the MDC ADMAX SHU is hardly surprising. However, the conditions to which the post-9/11 detainees were subjected were outrageously restrictive even for supermaximum-security confinement. An ADMAX SHU is rare in the federal system, because conditions in the regular SHU are generally considered to be suitably restrictive for even the most dangerous criminals. Prior to housing the post-9/11 detainees, MDC didn't even have an ADMAX SHU, and staff had to make quick changes to the existing SHU unit to prepare for the influx of the "dangerous" detainees.[17] Upon admission to the ADMAX SHU, the post-9/11 detainees were subjected to a complete communications blackout. The detainees were not allowed to make or receive telephone calls, nor could they send or receive mail. Moreover, the detainees' names were put on a special list, so that when loved ones or attorneys tried to visit the detainees at the facility, they were turned away and told that the detainee was not being held at that facility. Detainees had no way to contact their families to explain their situation; nor could they contact lawyers for assistance or advice. Reports differ on how long this initial communication blackout lasted, but the OIG report concludes that it was at least a few weeks, and quite possibly longer.

The harshness of their surroundings must have made this isolation almost unbearable. The detainees in the ADMAX SHU were placed alone, or sometimes with one or two cellmates in ten-by-six foot cells, for 23 to 24 hours a day. Many detainees complained that the cells were too cold, and they were forced to sleep without mattress or blanket, on a concrete slab with only a sheet. Their only opportunity for recreation required transportation, in handcuffs and shackles, to a freezing outdoor area, where they could exercise alone, from 5:30 am to 6:30 am. They were not provided with any recreation or exercise equipment. Many were denied soap, towels, reading materials, and reading glasses. Most of the detainees were unable to practice their religion, as prison officials denied them their holy books and approved foods, and refused to tell them the time, making proper prayer impossible.

When they were given attorney or family visits, after the communications ban was lifted, they were left in handcuffs and shackles, even though the visits were "no contact," and the thick Plexiglas rendered the restraints redundant. According to BOP regulations, they were to be given one social telephone call a month and one legal telephone call a week. However, many post-9/11 detainees complained that they weren't even given these limited opportunities.

Bureau of Prisons regulations require substantial procedural protections immediately after a detainee is placed in any form of administrative or disciplinary segregation.[18] Without reason or explanation, the BOP violated all of their own rules; prison administrators placed and retained the post-9/11 detainees in this restrictive confinement without any form of individualized review of their potential dangerousness.

The physical and verbal abuse to which the post-9/11 detainees were systematically subjected was also against regulation, but tacitly condoned. Of nineteen detainees interviewed by the OIG team, every single one complained of some form of abuse.[19] In interviews by the Center for Constitutional Rights, one detainee recalled being strip-searched and beaten by several guards upon his admission to MDC. The guards bent back his thumbs, stepped on his bare feet with their shoes, and pushed the man into the wall so hard that he fell to the floor. Guards kicked him in the face when he was on the floor, called him a "terrorist," and told him to expect rough treatment throughout his detention. Many other detainees reported similar physical beatings by guards who swore at them and denigrated their religion and ethnicity.

The systematic extent of this physical abuse was detailed in a second OIG report, released in December of 2003, which focused exclusively on abuse at MDC. According to the conclusions of the supplemental report, MDC staff and supervisors engaged in the following types of physical brutality: slamming, bouncing, and ramming detainees against the walls; bending detainees' arms, hands, wrists, and fingers (referred to by MDC staff as "goosenecking"); pulling and stepping on detainees' restraints to cause pain; improper use of restraints; and rough and inappropriate handling.[20] The incidents of abuse were far from sporadic. The OIG report conveys evidence that "*almost all* the detainees were slammed against walls," that at least "one officer *always* twisted detainees' hands," that some officers stepped on detainees' leg chains "*whenever* they were stopped," and that detainees were "*often* handled roughly and inappropriately."[21] Moreover, according to the OIG report, quite a few of these incidents either involved, or were brought to the attention of, senior MDC management.[22]

The abuse often took on a nationalistic flavor that is particularly disturbing. According to the supplemental report, many detainees complained that when they were first brought to MDC, guards pushed their face against a T-shirt that had been pinned up on the wall at the entrance to the facility.[23] The T-shirt had a picture of the American flag over the slogan THESE COLORS DON'T RUN.

Many of the OIG's conclusions were made possible by review of videotapes taken during detainee movements around the facility. These tapes contradicted statements by MDC staff about the treatment of the detainees and were originally withheld despite specific OIG requests.[24] MDC officials, including the warden, repeatedly failed to comply fully with the OIG's requests for these tapes.[25] Indeed, the tapes that provided most of the evidence of the above physical abuse were withheld from the OIG for over a year; they were only discovered when OIG officials visited MDC, and asked to see a storage room referred to by one MDC officer.[26] Upon entering the storeroom, the OIG staff saw, clearly marked, several boxes of tapes that had been omitted from the past requests. These long-suppressed tapes provided much of the evidence corroborating the detainees' allegation of physical abuse.[27]

Post-9/11 detainees classified as "of interest" or "interest undetermined" were lucky to avoid placement in the ADMAX SHU at MDC, but they, too, were confined in harsh and inappropriate conditions. Over half of the post-9/11 detainees were confined at Passaic County Jail, in Paterson, New Jersey. Passaic County Jail is located approximately 25 miles from the Bureau of Immigration and Customs Enforcement (ICE) (the new name for the INS after its reorganization into the Department of Homeland Security in March of 2003) Newark District Office in Paterson, New Jersey. The four-story facility was built in 1956 and has an official capacity of 839, but regularly holds more than double that number of detainees. According to the current sheriff's web page, it "has been deemed the most overcrowded jail in the state of New Jersey." The jail houses immigration detainees, state inmates and pretrial detainees, and US Marshal Service prisoners in medium- and high-security cells.

At Passaic County Jail, the post-9/11 detainees were held with other immigration detainees under unsafe and unnecessarily harsh conditions of confinement. Although the OIG Report concluded that conditions at Passaic were significantly less restrictive and less brutal than those at MDC, the Center for Constitutional Rights' own investigation revealed that post-9/11 detainees and regular immigration detainees spent at least 23 hours a day locked in dirty, overcrowded, and vermin-infested dorms so lacking in ventilation as to create a serious risk to the detainees' physical and mental well-being. Unlike MDC, Passaic did not isolate the post-9/11 detainees from other inmates and subject them to unusually restrictive conditions; instead the post-9/11 detainees at Passaic were subjected to the same unsanitary and punitive conditions as all the other unfortunate residents of that jail.

Detainees at Passaic, like those at MDC, had no opportunity for contact visitation with family members and friends, and limited access to the phone. They were only allowed to place collect calls, and at exorbitant rates. They spent their days packed into dorm-style cells, crowded with three-level bunk beds. The detainees were subjected to frequent late-night cell searches, during which guards with attack dogs would enter the room shouting, wake everybody up, and make them face the wall as the officers tore apart their bedding and personal belongings, searching for contraband. Throughout the winter, they had no access to outdoor recreation or direct sunlight. Food was unappetizing and served in stingy portions. Those detainees who were observant Muslims had little opportunity to engage in formal prayer and no access to halal meat. While the OIG did not find the same systemic abuse as reported at MDC, several post-9/11 detainees held at Passaic did complain to CCR staff of verbal and physical harassment similar to that experienced by the MDC detainees.

INDEFINITE AND PROLONGED DETENTION

In addition to the grueling conditions at the facilities in which the post-9/11 detainees were confined, the lengthy and indefinite nature of the detention in itself caused the post-9/11 detainees significant physical and emotional distress. Under the orders of the Justice Department, detainees were subjected to a "hold until cleared" policy. Noncitizens held in immigration detention under normal circumstances are often eligible for bond hearings, at which an immigration officer can oppose their bond request by arguing to an immigration judge that the detainee represents a flight risk or a danger to the community. If the individual is deemed deportable, the Bureau of Immigration and Customs Enforcement is required by statute to remove the noncitizen within 90 days of the final removal order.[28] However, according to officials in the FBI and the INS, the Justice Department ordered that all post-9/11 detainees be held until the FBI cleared them of any connection to terrorism. In order to hold these people, INS officers had to bend or break their own rules. INS officers opposed bond for all the post-9/11 detainees, even in cases where they had no access to evidence that the individual actually posed a flight risk or a danger to the community.[29] When forced to defend this position before an immigration judge, the immigration officer requested repeated continuances, to avoid having to admit that he or she had no evidence appropriate to oppose bond.[30] Moreover, rather than using the statutory period to prepare for the detainees' deportation, the INS held them for investigative purposes during this period, and did not even begin preparing travel documents and effectuating the deportation until after the clearance came through.

Despite the fact that it soon became clear to Justice Department officials that many of the detainees in custody had no connection to terrorism, the "hold until cleared" policy continued to be implemented across the board. The FBI clearance process took quite a long while. The average time period from day of arrest to day of clearance was 80 days, and for some detainees it took much longer; over a quarter of the clearances took over three months.[31] Ironically, the FBI's own awareness of the limited investigative value of the detainees prolonged their detention, as resources were diverted from the time-consuming clearance process to investigation of those individuals who were of "genuine investigative interest"—a category that did not apply to the vast majority of the post-9/11 detainees.[32]

LEGAL CHALLENGES TO THE POST-9/11 DETENTIONS

The mistreatment of the post-9/11 detainees described above, along with the current mistreatment of immigration detainees in general, raises many urgent constitutional questions, some of which are currently under litigation in the federal courts. This section will describe the legal challenges to the post-9/11 detentions and related policies and the statutory and constitutional arguments involved.

The secrecy surrounding the detentions has many legal implications. One of the first stop-gap efforts mounted by civil liberties groups after 9/11 was to try to find out who was being swept up and what was happening to them. In October of 2001, dozens of public-interest civil liberties and immigrant rights organizations filed Freedom of Information Act (FOIA) requests seeking the identities of the post-9/11 detainees, as well as the names of their attorneys and the date, location, and reason for their arrest and release.

FOIA is a federal law that allows individuals to ask the government for information about its actions. The government must release any information that is not classified or otherwise exempt from disclosure under the law. The Department of Justice refused to comply with the groups' FOIA request, so the groups filed suit in federal court in D.C. to try to force the government to release the information. In *Center for National Security Studies v. U.S. Department of Justice*,[33] Judge Gladys Kessler ordered the Department of Justice to release the detainees' names, but held that the government could withhold all the other information. The Department of Justice appealed this decision to the Circuit Court, the D.C. Circuit reversed Judge Kessler's order and ruled that the Department of Justice did not have to release the detainees' names.[34]

The D.C. Circuit Court agreed with the government that the material requested falls into an FOIA exemption that allows an agency to withhold "records or information compiled for law enforcement purposes, but only to the extent that the production of such law enforcement records or information . . . could reasonably be expected to interfere with enforcement proceedings."[35] The court based their decision, to a large degree, on the importance of deferring to the government on issues of national security. To come to this conclusion, they fell, hook, line, and sinker, for the government's unsubstantiated reports of the type of individuals who were actually detained:

> The clear import of the declarations is that many of the detainees have links to terrorism. This comes as no surprise given that the detainees were apprehended during the course of a terrorism investigation, and given that several detainees have been charged with federal terrorism crimes or held as enemy combatants. Accordingly, we conclude that the evidence presented in the declarations is sufficient to show a rational link between disclosure and the harms alleged.[36]

Amazingly, the court's decision crediting the government's security fears came two weeks *after* the release of the OIG report, described above, with its well-researched and carefully drawn conclusion that almost none of the post-9/11 detainees had any connection to terrorism. There was a strong dissent by Judge Tatel, who argued for the need to balance the government's important national security interests against the public's right to scrutinize the action of its government.[37] Judge Tatel called the court to task for their uncritical acceptance of the government's factual assumptions:

> Nothing in the record tells us how many of those 1,182 detainees have been charged with federal terrorism crimes or held as enemy combatants. What little information the record does contain, however, suggests that the number may be relatively small. A list of federally charged detainees attached to the government's motion for summary judgment reports that as of the time this suit was filed, only one detainee had been criminally charged in the September 11 attacks and only 108 detainees had been charged with any federal crime—primarily violations of antifraud statutes.[38]

On January 12, 2004, the Supreme Court denied the plaintiffs' request for review of the D.C. Circuit's opinion.[39] Unfortunately, the Supreme Court's refusal to hear the case means that the secrecy that has surrounded the post-9/11 detentions will continue.

The names of the detainees are not the only information the government has tried to withhold from the public. On September 21, 2001, in an order known as the Creppy Directive, Chief Immigration Judge Michael Creppy barred the public and the press from attending immigration hearings related to individuals detained by the INS who were classified as being of "special interest." The Creppy Directive ordered immigration judges to close these "special interest" hearings, barring family, visitors, and press, and also to avoid discussing the cases or disclosing any information about them, to the point of refusing to confirm or deny the fact that the hearing is even scheduled. While an immigration judge has the authority to order a hearing closed on the basis of individualized information about the specific detainee, the Creppy Directive went much farther and required judges to implement a blanket closure, without any individualized inquiry. The federal courts are in disagreement as to whether this blanket closure violates the First Amendment's guarantee of a free press.

In *Detroit Free Press v. Ashcroft*,[40] the Sixth Circuit Federal Court of Appeals ruled that the government could not ban reporters from attending immigration hearings unless the judge assigned to the case makes an individualized determination that secrecy is required, in that specific case, to protect national security. Judge Damon Keith, in striking down the government's position, characterized it as an attempt to

> take [the safeguard of a free press] away from the public by placing its actions beyond public scrutiny. Against noncitizens, it seeks the power to secretly deport a class if it unilaterally calls them "special interest" cases. The Executive Branch seeks to uproot people's lives, outside the public eye, and behind a closed door. Democracies die behind closed doors.... When a government begins closing doors, it selectively controls information rightfully belonging to the people. Selective information is misinformation.[41]

However, the Third Circuit Federal Court of Appeals examined the same issue and came to the opposite conclusion in *North Jersey Media Group v. Ashcroft*.[42] As with the withholding of the detainees' names, this decision is especially troubling when taken in conjunction with what we already know of the amorphous and random nature of the "of interest" designations described above and the way the secrecy of the detentions further paralyzed and fractured family and community relationships.

Finally, the most far-reaching legal challenge to the post-9/11 detentions is that brought by the Center for Constitutional Rights in its class action, *Turkmen v. Ashcroft*. The Center filed *Turkmen* in April of 2002, requesting damages and declaratory and injunctive relief on behalf of a class of male noncitizens from the Middle East and South Asia arrested after September 11, held on the pretext of minor immigration violations and detained for months. The Center amended the complaint in the summer of 2003 to reflect the greater detail and additional claims made apparent after the release of the OIG report.

The *Turkmen* case is a direct challenge to all of the aspects of the post-9/11 sweeps explained in the beginning of this chapter, including the arbitrary classification as "of interest" in the terrorism investigation; detention after the expiration of any valid immigration reason, without the procedural safeguards available to criminal detainees; the unnecessarily restrictive conditions of confinement and guard brutality; interference with the detainees' ability to practice their religion and access the courts; and the "hold until cleared" policy. The case is currently before Federal Court Judge John Gleeson of the Eastern District of New York. The named defendants, the United States, Attorney General John Ashcroft, FBI director Robert Mueller, former INS commissioner James Zigler, and the current and past wardens of MDC, have moved to dismiss the complaint on jurisdictional and qualified immunity grounds. Basically, the government defendants have argued that the sweeps were not illegal, and that even if they were, officials who acted "in good faith" cannot be punished for their wrongdoing. Judge Gleeson is expected to rule on this motion shortly.

THE POLICY AND SECURITY IMPLICATIONS OF FIGHTING TERRORISM THROUGH RACIAL PROFILING AND PRETEXTUAL USE OF THE IMMIGRATION LAW

While the OIG report leaves one with the implication that the post-9/11 detentions are over, immigration detention continues to be wielded as a tool of repression against disfavored groups in our society, and, as explained below, more sweeps seem likely in the event of another terrorist attack. For this reason, it is important to explore one final aspect of the post-9/11 detentions: the security and equality implications of the sweeps and the pretextual use of the immigration law to investigate terrorism.

The Justice Department has continually justified its actions as essential to preventing another terrorist attack in the wake of 9/11. While this is certainly an appropriate goal, the Department has failed to publicly quantify the utility or disutility of the sweeps and secret detentions. Certain conclusions can be drawn from the nature of the deportations themselves. Not a single individual swept up after 9/11 has been charged in connection to the September 11 attacks, and the overwhelming majority have been cleared not only of any connection to terrorism but also of any criminal activity whatsoever.

It is clear that the post-9/11 detentions were primarily based on racial profiling rather than individualized suspicion. "Racial profiling" is the use of race, religion, ethnicity, or national origin as a relevant factor in a law enforcement agent's decision to investigate a certain individual. It is not necessary for race, religion, ethnicity, or national origin to be the sole or determinative factor in a decision to initiate an investigation; it is enough if it plays any impermissible role.[43] As described above, initial FBI (and citizen informant) interest in individuals targeted post-9/11 was partially if not determinatively based on the particular individual's status or perceived status as an Arab, South Asian, or Muslim man. The anecdotal evidence is strong, yet we need not rely on it. According to the OIG report, detainees came from more than 20 countries, the vast majority of which are predominantly Arab or Muslim. The two most heavily represented countries were Pakistan and Egypt.[44]

While the terrorist attacks of 9/11 were arguably a unique and unprecedented criminal act, racial profiling as a crime-fighting technique is far from novel. African-Americans and Latinos have struggled against racial profiling, particularly in the context of pretextual traffic stops (leading to the popularly recognized "crime" of "driving while black or brown") for decades.[45] We can rely on some of the excellent scholarship undertaken in support of that continuing struggle to inform our understanding of the utility of racial profiling in the terrorism investigation. That scholarship and our understanding of the results of the post-9/11 sweeps show that a security policy based on racial profiling fails in terms of efficacy and morality.

The failure of racial profiling as a policy can be attributed to mistaken assumptions about criminal activity and law enforcement techniques. For example, in the context of profiling to fight the war on drugs, individuals who defend racial profiling do so based on the mistaken assumption that minorities commit the majority of drug offenses, such that concentrating law enforcement efforts on these individuals is simple common sense. This assumption is seriously flawed. Statistics show that African-American and Latino people use and sell drugs at a rate that is roughly proportionate to their percentage of the population. According to studies cited in one report, in the year 2000 African Americans represented 12 to 13 percent of the U.S. population and 11 percent of drug-users.[46] In that same year, Latinos represented 10 percent of drug users, and 13 percent of the U.S. population.[47] The percentage of minority drug sellers must also be roughly proportionate to their population, because we know that most drug users make purchases from members of their own racial or ethnic group.[48] Studies of the efficacy of racial profiling lead to similar conclusions. Traffic stops of minorities (presumably based, at least in part, on racial profiling) are equally or less likely to turn up evidence of drugs as stops of white people.[49] A related argument, that profiling works because minorities commit more violent crime than whites, ignores the fact that racial profiling is extremely rare in the violent crime context, since most victims of violent crime can provide police officers with a physical description of the perpetrator, which makes any profile unnecessary.

The second assumption that is relied on by people who support racial profiling is that so many minorities are criminals that random stops within their community are likely to lead to evidence of criminal activity. This argument is based on racist scapegoating and stereotyping that builds on an image of violent and threatening young black men—an image that was created during slavery to justify the continued enslavement and punishment of New Afrikan men. Of course, it is completely untrue—the vast majority of African-American and Latino people are law-abiding, just like the vast majority of white people.

The same assumptions fuel individuals who argue that racial profiling makes sense in the terrorism context. Not every terrorist before September 11 was an Arab, and it remains true that not every terrorist is Arab after September 11. After the Oklahoma City bombing, the second-worst act of terrorism ever committed against this country, law enforcement officials began searching for Arab and/or Muslim perpetrators based on this same mistaken understanding.[50] It is likely that this reliance on ethnic profiling delayed their identification of the actual culprit, Timothy McVeigh, a white American citizen. Similarly, in the time since September 11, 2001, it appears that the closest we have come to another plane-related attack was the attempt by Richard Reid, a British citizen of Jamaican descent, to ignite a bomb in his shoe while on an airplane midflight.

We can also see that just as using a pretext of traffic stops to search African-Americans and Latinos for drugs does not actually result in disproportionate evidence of drugs, neither does pretextual use of the immigration law to investigate Arab, Muslim and South Asian people result in evidence of any terrorist activity. This is clearly demonstrated by the failure of the post-9/11 sweeps to result in any convictions for terrorism-related offenses.

Members of a targeted population bear the burden of this racial profiling, as they are forced to undergo humiliating interactions with the police—stigmatized by popular perceptions of their criminality—and arrested and jailed (and in this case deported) at disproportionate levels. In this way, racial profiling not only fails to achieve significant law enforcement goals, it actually impedes effective law enforcement by engendering distrust of law officers in minority communities, thus making many law-abiding members of those communities less likely to cooperate with police investigations and less willing to report crimes when they are victimized. In fact, many city police departments across the country have opposed the federal government's attempt to use them to enforce immigration laws, as they know it will alienate them from immigrant communities and put stress on an already tense relationship. These cops also know that racial profiling casts too wide a net and thus diverts law enforcement resources from a thorough investigation of those individuals for whom there is an actual reason to suspect criminal activity.

Similarly, the pretextual use of the immigration law as a vehicle for racial profiling also impedes our security. The ease with which individuals can be detained for immigration violations and the use of such detention to facilitate the terrorism investigation shields this investigation from public scrutiny. This shield is multifaceted. Individuals in immigration detention are not provided lawyers, and this limits their ability to disseminate information about their situation to the public, as does the frequent end result of immigration detention: deportation. Moreover, in the post–9/11 context, judicial abdication and fear over national security has led to increased secrecy around these detentions. This secrecy, combined with the low threshold required under law to arrest (and eventually deport) an individual suspected of violating the immigration code, has allowed the Bush administration to create the impression that dangerous individuals are being arrested, detained, and deported, when in reality they are no closer to finding the terrorists among us. The public perception of effective law enforcement enables discriminatory and unjust actions even as it shields law enforcement agencies from public scrutiny and criticism. This leaves us all not only less free, but also less safe.

Unfortunately, while the OIG has done a very important public service in uncovering and detailing the excesses of the post-9/11 detentions, the OIG reports do not undertake a critical examination of the utility of racial profiling and pretextual use of immigration law to fight terrorism, as outlined above. In the initial OIG report, the inspector general made 21 recommendations to the Department of Justice and the Department of Homeland Security. The Department of Justice responded in writing with information on how, and to what degree, it intended to implement these recommendations. On September 5, 2003, the OIG released an analysis of those responses.[51] The Department of Justice replied with a second round of explanations and some policy changes, and this second round of responses was the subject of a January 5, 2004, report by the OIG.[52] Close analysis of these communications between the OIG and the Department of Justice leads to the unsettling conclusion that future detentions and sweeps are likely. The recommendations and the responses betray both parties' belief that, in the event of another terrorist attack, law enforcement will once again be justified in sweeping up noncitizens and detaining them under the authority of the immigration code.

For example, the OIG recommended that the Department of Justice institutionalize a system with set criteria to classify noncitizens arrested en masse in the event of another terrorist attack, in order to facilitate a faster clearance process by differentiating between noncitizens of varying levels of investigative interest.[53] The OIG suggested implementation of a checklist to standardize an FBI officer's investigation of any "illegal alien's potential connection to terrorism."[54] Such criteria "might" require "some level of evidence linking the alien to the crime or issues" involved.[55] The Department of Justice's initial response was supportive of the need for set criteria (although none were provided) but reiterated the following position:

> Even if the FBI possessed no specific information that a specific alien had ties to terrorism, if we were to experience another large-scale terrorist attack on U.S. soil, it is likely that the FBI would want to check with other agencies, both in the U.S. and abroad, before making a final determination that an alien arrested in connection with the investigation of such an attack in fact has no ties to terrorism.[56]

In their second response, after the OIG indicated that it did not find this initial response satisfactory, the Department of Justice reported the creation of the Terrorist Threat Integration Center (TTIC), which will maintain a database of information about terrorists and terrorist activities that can be mined for matches with a given noncitizen's name and information. Noncitizens detained in connection to a future terrorism investigation whose names do not give rise to any identifiable traces to anyone in the database will be cleared quickly, and will be eligible for a bond proceeding. Noncitizens with a match, *and* noncitizens without a match for whom "the nature of the subject's activity indicated that they were involved in the planning of, or participation in, a terrorist related activity," may be detained for further investigation.[57]

The OIG found this second response satisfactory[58] despite the fact that the back and forth does nothing to address the serious justice and security problems, raised above, with terrorism investigations based on racial profiling carried out by pretextual use of the immigration code. The Department of Justice's responses do not specify any level of proof or suspicion required to justify the initial or the continued detention. Moreover, the DOJ and OIG both start from the assumption that in the case of a terrorist attack, all noncitizens start out as suspects. Instead of continuing a critical examination of stated Department of Justice policy in the event of another terrorist attack, the OIG is now poised to ensure not the prohibition of future secret sweeps of noncitizens, but faster and more efficient sweeps the next time around.

CONCLUSION

The work of community organizers, civil libertarians, independent media, and the Office of the Inspector General have led to a commendable level of public outrage over governmental excesses in the wake of 9/11. However, this victory is incomplete. As this book goes to print, we are still awaiting an initial determination as to the legality of the sweeps in the *Turkmen* case, and public statements by the Department of Justice and ICE make clear those agencies' intent to continue to target noncitizens through use of the immigration law in the fight against terrorism. Noncitizens are under attack in the form of a wave of repressive new legislation further criminalizing violations of the immigration law, while more and more money is earmarked for policing and detention to the neglect of basic immigration services. These discriminatory policies and policing betray our devotion to equal protection under the law without providing quantifiable security returns. What instead has been created is an apartheid state for immigrants and noncitizens of color. For this reason, our struggle must not focus solely on the governmental abuses documented after 9/11, but also on the harsh and racist immigration system that continues to incubate such abuse.

NOTES

1   Alison Siskin, *Immigration-Related Detention: Current Legislative Issues*, CRS Report RL32369, April 28, 2004.
2   OIG report at 10–11.
3   Ibid. at 12.
4   Ibid. at 12.
5   Ibid. at 13.
6   Ibid. at 16.
7   Ibid.
8   Ibid. at 42.
9   Ibid.
10 OIG report at 18.
11 Ibid.
12 Ibid.
13 Jessica Gavora, "The Prisoners' Accomplice," *Policy Review*, September–October 1996, 79.
14 Ibid.
15 "USA: A Briefing for the UN Committee Against Torture," Amnesty International, 2000, 12.
16 Christian Parenti, *Lockdown America: Police and Prisons in the Age of Crises* (London: Verso), 2000.
17 OIG report at 119.
18 *See* 28 C.F.R. §, 541.22 (requiring certain procedures before and after detainees are placed in administrative segregation).
19 OIG report at 143.
20 Supp. OIG report at 16, 18, 20, 22, 25, 28.
21 Supp. OIG report at 10, 17, 21, 26 (emphasis added).
22 Ibid. at 22, 24, 25, 38.
23 Ibid. at 11.
24 Ibid. at 39–42.
25 Ibid. at 40–41.
26 Ibid.
27 Ibid.
28 8 U.S.C. § 1231.
29 OIG report at 78.
30 Ibid. at 81.
31 Ibid. at 46, 51.
32 Ibid. at 47.

33 215 F. Supp. 2d 94 (D.D.C. 2002).

34 331 F.3d 918 (D.C. Cir. 2003).

35 *Center for National Security Studies v. U.S. Department of Justice*, Ibid. at 925–26 (D.C. 2003) (citing 5 U.S.C. § 552 (b)(7)(A)).

36 Ibid. at 931.

37 Ibid. at 937.

38 Ibid. at 941.

39 *Center for National Security Studies v. Department of Justice*, 124 S. Ct. 1021 (2004).

40 303 F.3d 681 (6th Cir. 2002).

41 Ibid. at 683.

42 308 F.3d 198 (3d. Cir. 2002).

43 Race, religion, ethnicity, and national origin play a permissible role in law enforcement efforts when investigative decisions are made on the basis of an eyewitness description of a specific perpetrator that includes racial, religious, ethnic, or national origin characteristics.

44 The national origin of the detainees breaks down as follows: 254 from Pakistan; 111 from Egypt; and between 10 and 50 in descending order, from Turkey, Jordan, Yemen, India, Saudi Arabia, Morocco, Tunisia, Syria, Lebanon, and Israel. *See* OIG report at 21.

45 Of course, racial profiling is not limited to traffic stops, but also implicates the disproportionate sentencing and prosecution of the government's "war on drugs" and discriminatory stop-and-frisk techniques in communities of color. This profiling can be traced back to the Fugitive Slave Act of 1850, under which African-Americans (or New Afrikans) were stopped by whites demanding to see documentation that they were free, or had leave from the slaveholder.

46 *Wrong Then, Wrong Now: Racial Profiling Before & After September 11, 2001*, Leadership Conference on Civil Rights Education Fund, 17.

47 Ibid.

48 Ibid.

49 Ibid.

50 Ibid. at 27.

51 Analysis of Responses by the Department of Justice to Recommendations in the Office of the Inspector General's June 2003 Report on the Treatment of September 11 Detainees (December 2003). Available at: http://www.usdoj.gov/oig/igspecr1.htm.

52 Analysis of Second Response by the Department of Justice to Recommendations in the Office of the Inspector General's June 2003 Report on the Treatment of September 11 Detainees (January 2004). Available at: http://www.usdoj.gov/oig/igspecr1.htm.

53 Ibid. at 3.

54 Ibid.

55 Ibid.

56 Ibid. at 3–4.

57 Ibid. at 5–6.

58 Ibid. at 7–8.

10
Statement
Mohamed Maddy

Mohamed Maddy was a "special-interest" detainee picked up in the post-9/11 sweeps. He was held for over a year and a half in the infamous Metropolitan Detention Center and in Passaic County Jail before being deported to Egypt.

WITH MY RESPECT and my best regards, this is my story with the FBI and MDC [Metropolitan Detention Center]. Both of them lie, you can't know who to believe. I went to the USA on 24 August 1997. My plan was to stay in USA without papers, like millions of the people that are still in the USA. They are Spanish, Russian, Albanian, Pakistani, Brazilian, English, French, African, and from all over the world. Some people overstay, many people are smuggled in from Mexico, Cuba, or India through the ocean swimming or coming from San Diego.

I came to the USA on 24 August 1997, then my Egyptian wife and my sons came later. I decided to stay in the USA to educate my sons in the school and after high school we will come back to Egypt. In 22 September 2001 the FBI came to my job and they were asking me about my sons and they asked me about my wife—if I lived with her. I said yes, and they told me, "If we came to your house, we can find her with you." I said yes, but I was surprised about that, and I was scared. They started the investigation with me at 10:00 pm, and they took me to the FBI building and I spent there three hours or more. They were asking me about how I work in the airport. I saw one officer there was looking at me like a devil to scare me. Then they left me alone for two hours behind glass. Then they said you go home, but if we found you helped people get inside the USA for money, you will spend ten

171

years in jail. I said no, then I went home and my wife was crying for me.

Then the second day I went to my job. I hadn't sleep well. I was very tired and took permission to go back home. Then I went to my job another day and the FBI told my boss to fire me. The FBI were investigating me in the airport the same week.

On 2 October 2001, they came to my house around 5:00 pm. They wanted to talk to me, and I welcomed them and they started to search my house. Then they asked and I answered some questions, but they didn't ask me if they could search and then they didn't ask me if I wanted to answer or if I needed a lawyer. I gave them my passport and my driving license. Then they asked me about my wife's passport. My wife wasn't in the house because we were fighting two days before and she went to my friend's house. Then the FBI asked me about my American wife—I told them everything. We married for a green card only. They took my sons to my friend's house. I was scared and I asked where they would take my sons. They didn't answer me but they saw me crying and they told me, "We will take them to your friend's house." They asked me if I prayed and I said no. "Do you go to the mosque to pray?" I said sometimes. Then they asked me my feelings about September 11. I said the truth: that it was very bad because a lot of people died and everyone has friends who work in the World Trade Center. They took all the passports and the green card and all my IDs and they told me, we will leave you today, but don't move from here until tomorrow at 2:00 pm. We will ask our bosses if we come to catch you or not. Then they left and I spent the night without sleeping.

On 2 October 2001, at around 2:00 pm around 16 officers from the FBI came to my house. They think I'm a terrorist or a criminal but I was very polite and I was very strong. I was crying but you can ask any person in my position what he can do in this situation. They were searching my house again and they gave searching papers to sign, and I did sign. Then everybody left the house one by one until there were just three officers left. And they told me, now Mr. Maddy we will arrest you. Then they put a chain on my hand and my hands were behind me. I was telling them to please cover my hands because I didn't want my neighbors to see me like that. They put a blue shirt on my hands, then they put me in the car. They were asking me again if I need a lawyer and I said I need a lawyer.

They took me to the Marshall building in Brooklyn. Then they made identification and my registration number was 51487-054. I will never forget this number all my life. Then they took me to the Metropolitan Detention Center in Brooklyn. It was around 7:30 pm Wednesday, 3 October 2001. Then we waited until the gate opened and we went inside the jail, or the Hell that's what I like to say—then you can call it the Metropolitan Hell Center. Then I spent many hours with my hands chained behind me. Then the devils came. They were six officers—I saw them behind the window and two of them came and hung my hands. That was very bad. Then they took me to the wall and they put my face on the wall. One was behind me with his hand on my neck and his legs between my legs. Then one took my right hand and the other one took my left hand. Remember my hands were still behind me with the chain then. And they were wild animals. They took my glasses and they pushed me to the wall very hard, my shoulder started to hurt very bad. Then they took me down to the door. Then the wild dogs were hanging me from my arms and they were running and I was jumping with them. But then they open the door and they pushed me very strong inside and I was waiting for another door and they were pushing me very hard. The officers took me to the searching room and the lieutenant took me to a room on the hill. They pushed me into the room and they put my chest and my face to the wall and they started hitting me by hand and by legs. And they were carrying me and hanging me from my arms. The lieutenant kept swearing. I was trying to talk to him and they were telling me to shut up your fucking mouth and don't turn around and they punish me from the back and they were punish me very hard and they were pushing me to the wall very very hard and I was taking this all on my arm, until my arm became red and after two hours became dark blue. They were carry me from my hands and my arms and pushing me to the wall again until my mouth was bleeding. The lieutenant told me listen motherfucker, if you don't listen to me I will make you die. That means he will kill me. I thought I'm in Israel or Cuba or Iraq or another country not the USA. All the world was turning around me. I was feeling sweaty and dizzy and suddenly I didn't feel my feet and fell. And the officers were hanging me, they were wild animals. They were catching me very bad and suddenly they put me to the wall again and they told me put your face to the wall and they gave me a paper and the lieutenant asked me to sign it and I asked him how I sign the paper when you have my glasses and my hands in the back and I don't know what this paper. And he told me listen fuck you and he gave me the pen and he said sign here and he put my hand with the pen on the place I have to sign.

They give me order to turn myself to face them and they told me don't look to anybody and they start to unlock the chain and I was free from 2:00 pm to around 9:00 or 10:00 pm. Then they told me take your clothes off and I did one by one starting with T-shirt and ending with my underwear. I try to tell them that's no good because I'm Muslim. They said ha and hurry up and I did. Another lieutenant told me you are not going to see your clothes again and I felt very bad at this moment. They start to give me the jail uniform, the orange uniform—now I hate this color and I hate everything that reminds me about this jail. And they start to lock me up again. They put the chain around my feet and we start the long trip. They make me walk very fast and they were dragging me by my hands and running. I couldn't run but they were dragging me and when I was running one of the officers step down on the chain which was between my legs and I fell down. Then they took me to the elevator to the ninth floor. They put me in the cell number 919 for one hour and that was around 11:30 pm. Then I heard two Egyptian people talking and I heard Ahmed, and Khaled then Aziz, Sherif, Sa'id, Fatih, Hassan, Rafat, Salim, and Pakistani people, Ghani Abdurrahman, another Ghani, Islam Mohammed, and after one week another Mohammed came, then Da'ud Abdulhaqq. Then after one hour, I was feeling very bad and the lieutenant came to tell everybody to shut up and the lieutenant put Ahmed with me in my cell. We started talking and he asked me about my crime and I asked him about his crime. His crime was overstay, that's all. All this time I didn't eat and I wasn't feeling hungry but I was feeling scared and I feel dying and my arm started to hurt me. Then Ahmed asked me about it and I told him what the officers did with me and he told me they did the same with him. Then I slept at around 2:00 pm, and they woke me up at 5:00 am and I went to court at 8:00 am. They took me to the court and I found Julie Buckner, the lawyer. She came and told me "I'm your lawyer and I will sit with you before the court time." Then I told her what the officers did with me and I showed her the bruise on my arm. She was surprised and she told me when the judge asks you if you are guilty say no. When I went in front of the judge I said the same. Then she told the judge about what happened to me in MDC and she asked me to show him my arm and the bruise and another asked me to show him my bruise and another lawyer from legal aid or from the media was sitting in the court and they asked for a camera. And the court said we don't have a camera. Then one said I will buy a camera and they took a picture of me in the court with my bruise.

At MDC I was in the special housing, two or one in the cell and this was high security. The lights were turned on 24 hours a day, the shower was inside the cell, the water and the bathroom also. There were two beds in the cell. The officers were carrying many chains when they walked and they made high noise and talking and laughing and they were smoking also and we know it is not allowed in federal. Sometimes they cut cold water from the cells and I was drinking hot water. They shut off the air-conditioning and when we ask they say we don't have air-conditioning. It's very hot outside. That was in October and November and when the cold weather started they turned on the air-conditioning and made it very high. We were very cold and had to cover ourselves with two blankets. The food was very bad, it is not enough for children what about big men like us. All the inmates lose weight in the high-security unit. The breakfast was 5:00 am the lunches at 11:30 am and the dinner at 5 pm. I bought a radio from the commissary and after 2 weeks they take the radio back and they say it is not allowed in the special housing.

We were moved from cell to cell twice a week and they put Ahmed with his brother Khaled and they moved me with another person. During these days I was trying to call my sons and I couldn't because the counselor was very bad. The first social call I made was in November 13, 2001, after 45 days. When I made this call I was crying to send glasses for me and she did and they were returned back to her. I was angry, I needed my glasses, I wanted to read the Koran. And the officers would throw out the Koran like any other book and we were mad about that. I felt bad and one time I want to kill myself and after one hour they took me to another cell alone and they took all my clothes off and they gave me a hard jacket. I spent 24 hours in this cell with them watching me 24 hours. Then they put me with a person from Iraq. And when he came he told me "I was trying to kill myself and I put the sheet around my neck and I tied the sheet on the upper bed and I jumped and the officers came after that" and they put him in another cell watching him 24 hours for 2 weeks. I was try to let my sons and my wife come visit me and I have to prove she is my wife and I told them, she is in the passport, but had to bring the marriage certificate and translate it into English and send it to me. And she did that and she came to visit me the first time in the end of December. And if she came to visit me the time between 5:00 and 8:00 pm she has to come at 3:00 pm and wait downstairs till they call her then she goes to the ninth floor and waits for me in the visit room, glass between us and the video camera also. Then they call me after one hour she was waiting for me. And 4 officers brought me to the visiting room and the chain around my waist and my wife. They show my wife how I look. That's no good—I'm human, they are not supposed to do that. I didn't see my sons because is not allowed for children.

I write a letter to the captain and I asked him why I'm in the high-security unit. I met a lot of inmates in the court and their crimes were drugs and killings and they are in the general population. He answered me after two weeks and said you are still under investigation and we can't move you to general population. Then I write another letter to the warden and he said the same and said I have to be cleared by the FBI and we went to court and the lawyer asked the judge to remove me from high security to general population. He said, I don't have the power to do that. Then I went back to the jail. Then in January, the lawyer told me, Mohamed you will move to the general population soon and in January 24, 2002, I went to the general population and I was very happy because that is a different life in the high-security unit. I can make one phone call every month, only 10 minutes. But in general population I can call every day and any time. Then around January 28, 2002 my sons came to visit me for the first time and I was very happy. This was the first time to see them in 4 months. I can't tell you my feelings.

Then when I was in the general population I met one officer from the government—he was asking me about what happened to me in MDC and I told him everything and he told me, "We will need your cooperation when you go to Egypt to come here in the USA as a witness in this case because these officers they have to go to another job." But I want to tell you something, I don't like to go to the USA the rest of my life, and I will advise anyone don't go to the USA.

Then on April 4, 2002, I went to Court and the Federal Judge said time served and you will be deported to your country and don't come here again. I wanted to tell him I don't like your country, I wasn't happy in your country and I'm never go to your paradise and you too, don't come to my country. They told me don't come to the USA for 10 years.

11
What Does It Mean To Be An "Enemy Combatant"?

Barbara Olshansky

> "History teaches that grave threats to liberty often come
> in times of urgency, when constitutional rights seem too
> extravagant to endure…[But] when we allow funda-
> mental freedoms to be sacrificed in the name of real or
> perceived exigency, we invariably come to regret it."
> —*Skinner v. Railway Labor Executives' Association*, 489 U.S.
> 602, 635 (1989) (Marshall and Brennan, JJ., dissenting)

WHAT HAPPENS WHEN the president of the United States asserts
that he has the power to declare that you, an American citizen, are
an "enemy combatant" and order the military to arrest you, hold
you incommunicado, in solitary confinement, indefinitely, without charge or trial? While this might sound like it could never—
or at least would never—happen in this country, it is exactly what
happened to at least two citizens, Jose Padilla and Yaser Hamdi. This
chapter analyzes the use of the president's newly claimed power
and assesses whether there is any basis in U.S. or international law
for the exercise of such power. Specifically, we will be looking at
the following issues: (1) whether the president's constitutional
commander-in-chief power permits him to order the indefinite
detention without trial of American citizens; (2) whether this
power or international law authorizes him to detain indefinitely
noncitizens caught in a zone of military hostilities or those
arrested in countries far from any battlefield; (3) how the government has defined—or failed to define—the conduct that might

place a person at risk of falling within the new category of "enemy combatants"; and (4) what it means that the executive branch has exercised this power.

These questions not only call for a recalibrated balance between individual liberties and national security, they also frame a debate of historic dimension about this country's commitment to the rule of law. At the heart of this debate is the most fundamental question of our time: whether we are a nation ruled by laws—the written principles adopted by the people to provide a just, reasonable, and public guide for our conduct—or a nation ruled by men under whom no legal rights are guaranteed, where instead the governing principles are left to the good intentions of presidents and generals.

As the Bush administration's argument in the *Hamdi* and *Padilla* cases—and its action with regard to the Guantánamo detainees—plainly shows, the executive branch has taken the position that the president has the unilateral power to change the very foundations of our democracy. The government claims that the President's authority as commander in chief of the armed forces includes the power to capture "enemy combatants" *wherever* they are found, including within our nation's borders, and to detain them indefinitely, without permitting any court to review the president's actions.

Under the Bush administration's view, people detained pursuant to this power no longer have their First Amendment right of access to a court, their Fourth Amendment protection against unreasonable searches and seizures, their Fifth Amendment right to a lawyer, their Eighth Amendment protection against cruel and unusual punishment, or their constitutional right to petition a court for a writ of habeas corpus to challenge the legality of their detention. These are among the constitutional guarantees that we all understand form the pillars of justice and freedom sustaining our commitment to democracy.

For noncitizens detained as "enemy combatants," the situation is equally, if not more, dire; they have been denied all constitutional protections as well as all of the protections that they are owed—and which they properly would be accorded by other administrations—under international humanitarian law and international human rights law. They have, furthermore, been subject to detention and interrogation in the harsh conditions of the naval facility in Guantánamo Bay, Cuba.

A closer look at the *Hamdi* and *Padilla* cases reveals the deep division that now exists between those who advocate for the vesting of this unprecedented power in the president and those who believe that indefinite executive detention without judicial review is inimical to our commitment to the democratic principles of freedom and justice.

WHO OR WHAT IS AN "ENEMY COMBATANT"?

Unfortunately, from the Bush administration's first use of the phrase "enemy combatant" in 2001 through the present, no progress has been made in ascertaining the definition of this new status. Despite the vigorous efforts of federal legislators, civil rights organizations, international human rights organizations, and others, the government has continued to use the "enemy combatant" designation in many different ways to achieve numerous different ends.

Although in the *Hamdi* case the government claimed that it had developed a set of criteria that govern its determination of who receives "enemy combatant" status, no such guidelines have ever been made available to the public or even to the attorneys for Hamdi or Padilla. As a result, it is impossible for us to know who in the executive branch participates in the decision to designate a person as an "enemy combatant," what factors are considered when the decision is made, what evidence is required to support the decision, what standard of proof is used to assess that evidence, who reviews the assessment and under what standard, and how the decision is made to prosecute the person in the criminal justice system (as was the case for John Walker Lindh, the accused Taliban fighter) or transfer him to military custody for indefinite executive detention.

Indeed, the term "enemy combatant," as it is used by the Bush administration, does not fit within any category of participants in military hostilities as those categories are defined under international humanitarian law.[1] International humanitarian law—also known as "the laws of war"—is comprised of the rules agreed upon by the international community that govern conduct related to military hostilities. Under international humanitarian law, the term "enemy combatant"—although it is not frequently used by those knowledgeable in the field—has historically referred to a person who is fighting for the opposite side in military hostilities.[2] "Combatants" are "members of the armed forces of a Party to a conflict" who fight openly for one side in the conflict.[3] "Combatants" may not be prosecuted for the actions they lawfully take against members of the military forces of the opposing party; in a sense, they are deemed "privileged" to engage in combat activities by virtue of their membership in the armed forces of a party to the conflict. "Combatants" thus have the right to participate directly in hostilities.

International humanitarian law uses the term "unlawful combatants" to draw a distinction between the civilian population and the "combatants" in an armed conflict. The category of "unlawful combatants" includes two sets of people: (1) members of regular armed forces who do not wear uniforms and do not openly bear arms, and have consequently lost their privileged combatant status; and (2) civilians who unlawfully participate directly in battle and have never had privileged combatant status from the outset.[4]

Under international humanitarian law, both lawful and unlawful combatants are entitled to well-established substantive and procedural rights. According to the Geneva Conventions,[5] one of the main sources of law governing the manner in which wars between countries may be conducted, captured enemy soldiers, or "enemy combatants," are entitled to be treated as prisoners of war and must be treated in accordance with the safeguards and protections specified in the Conventions.[6]

The Geneva Convention Relative to the Treatment of Prisoners of War (the Third Geneva Convention) states that a person arrested in or near the battlefield has a right to be treated as a prisoner of war (POW) unless and until his status—or his innocence—has been determined by a "competent tribunal."[7] Because the United States has ratified all four Geneva Conventions, it has made them the supreme law of the land, and the federal government is legally bound to comply with them.[8] Furthermore, the U.S. military has adopted regulations that expressly incorporate the competent tribunal requirement of the Third Geneva Convention.[9] The military regulations delineate the procedures governing Geneva Convention hearings before competent tribunals, specifying that a panel of three commissioned officers will determine an individual's status based on a majority vote of the panel, using the preponderance of the evidence standard. The regulations further guarantee the detainees' right to attend the hearing, present witnesses, and address the panel.[10] According to the Bush administration, however, people declared by the president to be "enemy combatants," like Padilla and Hamdi, are not entitled to such procedures and instead may be held indefinitely without any process.[11] Nor are the "enemy combatants" detained in Camp Delta in the Guantánamo Bay Naval Station entitled to such procedures, according to the government. Thus, while the government invokes the laws of war and refers to "the settled wartime authority of the commander in chief to capture and detain enemy combatants" as the source and justification for the Executive's power to detain Padilla, it paradoxically refuses to comply with the requirements of the Geneva Conventions that comprise the core of these laws of war.[12]

THE CASE OF JOSE PADILLA

Jose Padilla is an American citizen. He was born in Brooklyn, New York, in 1971. On May 8, 2002, Padilla traveled on a commercial airliner from Pakistan to Chicago to visit his son, carrying a valid U.S. passport. Because he was arriving from a trip overseas, upon disembarking at O'Hare International Airport, Padilla proceeded to customs along with the other passengers on his flight. However, unlike the other travelers on the same flight, Padilla was asked to step aside by law enforcement officers and was immediately arrested.

We now know that Padilla was arrested on the authority of a material witness warrant issued by a federal court in New York in response to a request from the Justice Department. (A material witness warrant is a court order intended to ensure that witnesses who may have relevant information are available to testify before grand juries investigating federal crimes.)

Padilla was flown to New York late in the evening on May 14, 2002. He was taken to the high-security floor of the Metropolitan Correction Center (MCC). The next day, Padilla was brought before the federal district court in leg irons, shackles, and handcuffs. In court, Padilla and his appointed lawyer were permitted to review the affidavit that had been submitted in support of the material witness warrant. For the next several weeks, appointed counsel met with Padilla and filed papers on his behalf, seeking his release on the ground that a material witness could not be lawfully detained. Padilla's attorney anticipated receiving the court's decision on this request at a court conference scheduled for June 11, 2002. That conference never took place.

Instead, on Sunday, June 9, 2002, President George W. Bush filed a declaration with the court stating that Padilla was an "enemy combatant" and ordering the secretary of defense to take Padilla into custody. Padilla's appointed counsel was not notified of this Sunday conference at the court. Padilla was immediately taken into military custody and flown to the Naval Consolidated Brig in Charleston, South Carolina, where he remains today.[13] He has been held incommunicado and in solitary confinement since his initial designation as an "enemy combatant," without being charged with any crime and without being allowed access to family, friends, or the court. Although the court ordered the government to permit Padilla to meet twice with his appointed counsel, these meetings have been monitored by the government, and Padilla's attorneys have been under court order not to raise certain matters with Padilla. Under these circumstances, Padilla could not speak freely with his attorneys and therefore was unable to assist them in any way in mounting his defense. The government has not explained why Padilla, who was *already* being held in a secure facility by order of a civilian court when he was declared an "enemy combatant," needed to be detained by the military.

The presidential declaration of Padilla's "enemy combatant" status was supported only by a single sworn statement. Michael H. Mobbs, a special advisor to the undersecretary of defense for policy, submitted a declaration in support of the president's declaration and the military custody order. According to the Mobbs Declaration, Mobbs had no personal knowledge of any facts concerning Jose Padilla. All of his information was based on hearsay—on Mobbs's review of what he apparently considered to be the relevant records and reports about Padilla. Furthermore, Mobbs acknowledged in a footnote in his declaration that the two confidential sources that he relied on for his conclusions were two people held by the government who (1) "have been involved with al Qaeda for several years," including the group's terrorist activities; (2)

"have not been completely candid about their association with al Qaeda and their terrorist activities"; (3) have provided uncorroborated information; and (4) may have been "part of an effort to mislead or confuse U.S. officials."[14] Moreover, the Mobbs Declaration states that one of these two sources subsequently recanted some of the information provided, and the other source was "being treated with various types of drugs" during his interrogation.[15] In any other legal context, a declaration like the one submitted by Mobbs in support of Padilla's executive detention in a military brig would not have been permitted to be relied upon as evidence in court.

On the basis of the secondhand, uncorroborated, and unreliable information he reviewed, Mobbs stated in his declaration that Padilla moved to Egypt in 1998, traveled to Pakistan "in 1999 or 2000," and "also traveled to Saudi Arabia and Afghanistan."[16] The Mobbs Declaration makes clear that the government has no basis to allege that Padilla is a member of al Qaeda or that he took any steps in furtherance of any planned criminal activity. No allegations are made that Padilla participated in the September 11 attacks or in any other terrorist or criminal act against the United States or that he took up arms against the United States on behalf of any foreign army or terrorist organization. The Mobbs Declaration is silent as to the definition of "enemy combatant" status and as to what level of "association" or affiliation with al Qaeda is necessary to warrant treatment by the government as an "enemy combatant."

Padilla has been charged with *no* criminal or military offense. And the secretary of defense has stated that the government has no intention of ever charging Padilla with any crime. Indeed, the government has made clear that it is keeping him in military custody solely for interrogation purposes. This fact was made clear in the declaration submitted to the district court on January 9, 2003, by Vice Admiral Lowell E. Jacoby, director of the Defense Intelligence Agency. The Jacoby Declaration reveals the fact that Padilla is not being held as an "enemy combatant" because of any offenses that he has committed or any plans that he has made, but rather because "[his] potential intelligence value [is] very high."[17] As Admiral Jacoby makes clear, Padilla is being held in indefinite detention without any due process *solely* because he may have information that the government may be interested in at some point—any point—in the future. Admiral Jacoby indicates that the government fully intends to detain Padilla indefinitely because the "intelligence cycle is continuous," and "[t]here is a constant need to ask detainees new lines of questions as additional detainees are taken into custody."[18]

Neither the Constitution, nor Congress, nor any court in this country has ever approved such an abuse of executive authority. Detention for investigative purposes has never been a constitutionally sanctioned practice in America. That the detention of American citizens and their labeling as "enemy combatants" have occurred without so much as a nod in the direction of due process makes this radical departure from the rule of law all the more egregious and startling.

Moreover, our concern should be even greater here because the government's justification for Padilla's detention under solitary confinement conditions—conditions permitted only for those who commit serious crimes while already incarcerated—is that providing him with access to family or counsel may "threaten the perceived dependency and trust between [Padilla] and [the] interrogator." Elaborating on this justification, Admiral Jacoby stated:

> Only after such time as Padilla has perceived that help is not on the way can the United States reasonably expect to obtain all possible intelligence information from [him].... Providing him access to counsel now would create expectations by Padilla that his ultimate release may be obtained through an adversarial civil litigation process.[19]

In this regard, the Jacoby Declaration implies that seven months of incarceration (the length of Padilla's detention at the time the Jacoby Declaration was submitted) is not a sufficient amount of time to convince Mr. Padilla of the hopelessness of his situation.

By imprisoning Padilla *without a hearing of any sort* and *without producing any evidence against him*, the executive branch has taken one of the most drastic steps in our nation's history. It has ordered the arbitrary and indefinite detention of an American citizen, subjected him to drastic conditions of imprisonment, and thrown away the keys to the prison. Such action violates our constitutional guarantees and speaks loudly of official disregard for the moral values embodied in those guarantees. It fundamentally weakens the backbone of democratic civilization: the rule of law.

The government's unprecedented action poses a grave threat to the constitutional rights of all American citizens. The government seeks to strip from those it labels "enemy combatants" the protections ordinarily afforded to all citizens under the Bill of Rights of the Constitution. The government's argument that the president has this new power because the "war on terrorism" demands it amounts to the sweeping proposition that, with no meaningful judicial review, any American citizen alleged to be an "enemy combatant" can be detained indefinitely without charges or counsel simply on the government's say-so.

THE CASE OF YASER HAMDI

Like Jose Padilla, Yaser Esam Hamdi is a U.S. citizen; he was born on September 26, 1980, in Baton Rouge, Louisiana, and was raised in Saudi Arabia. The unclassified information concerning Hamdi indicates that he had traveled to Afghanistan from Pakistan on July 15, 2001, to do volunteer humanitarian relief work. He was arrested in September 2001 and held by U.S. forces in Afghanistan until

January 11, 2002, when he was transported with 384 other captives to Camp X-Ray, Guantánamo Bay, Cuba.[20] When it was discovered that Hamdi's claim of American citizenship was true, he was transferred on April 6, 2002, to a military jail in Norfolk, Virginia.

Since the beginning of his detention, Hamdi has never been charged with any offense and has been denied access to an attorney and the courts. Taking the same position as in the Padilla case, the government maintains that it has the authority to detain Hamdi indefinitely, incommunicado, without ever subjecting him to prosecution—civilian or military—solely because it has declared him an "enemy combatant."

According to the government, Hamdi went to Afghanistan at some point before September 2001. He was still present in Afghanistan after the United States and coalition forces subsequently began military operations in that country. The Northern Alliance captured him and turned him over to U.S. forces. The government maintains that Hamdi was "affiliated" with Taliban forces, and that at the time of his capture he was carrying a firearm that he turned over to Northern Alliance forces.[21]

In Afghanistan, the Northern Alliance held Hamdi in two different prisons. At the second prison, a U.S. interrogation team interviewed him. Thereafter, a U.S. military officer ordered his transfer to a U.S. detention facility in Kandahar, Afghanistan. After another "military screening" in January 2002, Hamdi was sent to the naval base at Guantánamo Bay, Cuba. In April 2002, based on records demonstrating Hamdi's U.S. citizenship, the government removed him from Guantánamo Bay, separating him from other persons captured in Afghanistan.[22]

As is the case with Padilla, Hamdi's designation as an "enemy combatant" is supported by a declaration submitted by Michael Mobbs.[23] Mobbs does not indicate that he has any personal knowledge of any facts concerning Hamdi's capture or detention. All of his knowledge is hearsay derived from a review of what he considers to be relevant records and reports.[24] Although Mobbs maintains in his declaration that he has been substantially involved with detainee operations since mid-February 2002, the *Federal Register* indicates that his position was not created until April 24, 2002.[25] Hamdi had already been detained and transferred to Norfolk by that time.

The Mobbs Declaration states that Hamdi traveled to Afghanistan in July or August 2001, prior to the attacks of September 11, and that he became "affiliated" with a Taliban military unit prior to the September 11 attacks on the United States.[26] The declaration further states that Hamdi received weapons training prior to September 11, but does not say from *whom* the training was received, *where* it was received, or *what* the training consisted of. According to Mobbs, Hamdi remained with the Taliban after the September 11 attacks and after October 7, 2001, when the United States began military operations against the Taliban. The Mobbs Declaration does not identify the Taliban unit that Hamdi was allegedly affiliated with, nor does it state whether this unit wore uniforms or what functions the unit served. No further details are provided.

The Mobbs Declaration reports that on an unspecified date in late 2001, Northern Alliance Forces were engaged in battle with the Taliban. Mobbs does not say that the Taliban unit with which Hamdi had "affiliated" was engaged in battle with the Northern Alliance. While Mobbs says that Hamdi's unit surrendered to Northern Alliance forces, he does not say where or when this occurred or what activity Hamdi was engaged in at that time. According to the Mobbs Declaration, at the time of the unit's surrender, Hamdi apparently was allowed to keep his weapon, which would seem to indicate that the Northern Alliance did not expect him to try to escape.[27] Later, while being transported from Konduz to Mazar-e-Sharif, Afghanistan, Hamdi was directed to surrender his weapon to Northern Alliance forces. After a prison uprising in Mazar-e-Sharif, Hamdi was transferred by Northern Alliance forces to a prison at Sheberghan, Afghanistan. which was also under the control of Northern Alliance forces. There is no allegation that Hamdi took part in the prison uprising.[28]

While he was in the custody of Northern Alliance forces, Hamdi was interviewed by a U.S. interrogation team. According to Mobbs, Hamdi identified himself to the U.S. interrogation team "as a Saudi citizen who had been born in the United States and who entered Afghanistan the previous summer to train with and, *if necessary*, fight for the Taliban." The Mobbs Declaration does not elaborate on what Hamdi allegedly meant by "if necessary."

While portions of the Mobbs Declaration refer to the terrorist group al Qaeda, nowhere in the declaration does Mobbs assert or even suggest that Hamdi was a member of al Qaeda.

The only definition of the term "enemy combatant" in the Mobbs Declaration is as follows: "individuals associated with al Qaeda or Taliban who were and continue to be enemy combatants."[29] The Declaration says that based upon interviews of Hamdi, he was considered to be an enemy combatant by a U.S. military screening team, which determined that Hamdi met the criteria for "enemy combatants" over whom the United States was taking control, and that he also met the criteria for transfer to Guantánamo Bay, Cuba. These screening criteria, and the reasons why Hamdi met them, are not set forth in the declaration. The declaration finally asserts that a "subsequent interview of Hamdi confirmed that he surrendered and gave his firearm to Northern Alliance Forces, which supports his classification as an enemy combatant."[30]

The Mobbs Declaration does not offer any factual support or explanation for Hamdi's current detention in solitary confinement in the naval brig in Norfolk. It is silent on why he was separated from all other detainees at Guantánamo Bay and then moved to his current location. Further, the Mobbs Declaration does not set forth facts or determinations made by others that would support treating Hamdi as if he were an unlawful combatant.[31] Finally, the Mobbs Declaration does not provide any factual basis for the notion that granting Hamdi's counsel access to him would pose any problems for national security or would interfere with United States intelligence-gathering efforts in any way. No reason is given for placing Hamdi in military custody.

Padilla's and Hamdi's confinement in indefinite executive detention as "enemy combatants" contrasts greatly with the government's decision to prosecute John Walker Lindh, an American citizen who was arrested while fighting for the Taliban government on the battlefield in Afghanistan. Lindh was prosecuted in the criminal justice system rather than remanded to indefinite detention.[32] As the differential treatment of these individuals makes clear, the government has established a malleable category—the undefined rubric of "enemy combatant" status—that may be molded at will so as to include anyone deemed guilty of a range of "offenses" from specific, statutorily defined military offenses, to crimes, to inchoate speculations about an individual's intention to act at some point in the future.[33] In fact, even the small survey of designations discussed above indicates that the definition of "enemy combatant" may cover a wide spectrum of activities, from fighting for foreign armies against the United States to merely contemplating the commission of criminal acts within this country's borders. Furthermore, the decision to treat so differently individuals such as Hamdi and Lindh, apprehended in apparently similar circumstances, indicates the presence not only of wholly unfettered discretion but also the arbitrary exercise of such discretion.

THE CIRCUMSTANCES OF THE GUANTÁNAMO DETAINEES

As we have seen in the cases of two American citizens arrested under vastly different circumstances (one ostensibly swept up somewhere near the military hostilities in Afghanistan and one arrested in Chicago), little can be divined about the likelihood of being declared an "enemy combatant" based on one's alleged role in the war in Afghanistan. In fact, there is yet another ill-defined group subject to this declaration. The Bush administration has stated that all of the people being detained by the U.S. military in the Guantánamo Bay Naval Station in Cuba are "enemy combatants" as well.

A veil of secrecy surrounds the prison and its inmates. The government has never publicly acknowledged who the detainees are that are being held at Guantánamo. Indeed, the government has never disclosed information regarding any particular detainee, including the circumstances of his seizure, what the government believes he may have done to justify his continued detention, or his current welfare.

While little is known about the detainees being held at Guantánamo, some information has come to light through the public testimony of detainees' family members and the statements of consular officials who have had limited contact with the Guantánamo detainees.[34] The situation of this group of "enemy combatants" is best illustrated by taking a look at the circumstances of several people whose family members brought the case *Rasul v. Bush*[35]—which challenged of the Bush administration's decision to hold the Guantánamo detainees without providing a Geneva Convention tribunal to determine their status or any other court review of their detention.

As discussed in chapter 2, the people incarcerated in Camp Delta at Guantánamo Bay were arrested in a number of different contexts. International and domestic law dictates how people arrested in these different circumstances must be treated. For example, under international humanitarian law governing the conduct of war, individuals fighting for the Taliban government who were arrested on or near the battlefield should have been accorded

POW status, had the government convened a Geneva Convention tribunal as required. Because the Taliban was the effective government of Afghanistan at the start of the war, and both Afghanistan and the United States are parties to the Geneva Conventions of 1949, the armed attacks by the United States and other nations against the Taliban constitute an international armed conflict to which the Geneva Conventions and customary international humanitarian law apply. In contrast, because al Qaeda is a clandestine organization comprised of people and groups from many countries and holds no sovereign territory, it lacks an international legal personality. Because it is not a nation state, al Qaeda cannot be a party to the Geneva Conventions. Al Qaeda 's members are not entitled to be combatants under international law, and the organization's members who engage in terrorist activities are properly subject to trial and punishment under national criminal laws. Those persons who are not members of the Taliban's armed forces are civilians, and as such they are not privileged by law to take part legally in hostilities.[36] Thus, civilians who engage in combat activities must be tried as criminals in civilian courts as well.

Although these categories would seem to cover the universe of those who have been sent to and held at Guantánamo Bay, they do not. Amongst the detainees in Camp Delta are people, like Jamil El-Banna and Bisher Al-Rawi, two British citizens who were arrested in The Gambia while they were on a business trip to that country to begin the development of a peanut oil manufacturing facility. Neither of these individuals has ever been to Afghanistan or Pakistan and neither took part in any military action against the United States. Nevertheless, both are imprisoned at Guantánamo.

Both of these individuals were allowed to write a letter to their respective families, which the International Committee of the Red Cross (ICRC) delivered. When their families learned that they were in custody, they contacted attorneys. The attorneys and family members for the two men have repeatedly implored the United States to provide information regarding their welfare, and to let them speak with the detainees. These entreaties have gone unanswered. Apart from sporadic, censored mail from their families, the detainees have had no contact with the outside world.

El-Banna and Al-Rawi have not been charged, and they have not appeared before any military or civilian tribunal. The government contends they need *not* be informed of their rights under domestic or international law. The government also claims that they are not entitled to the protections of the Geneva Conventions. At the same time, government officials have acknowledged that at least some of the detainees at Guantánamo were victims of circumstance and are probably innocent.[37]

The government has, however, "allowed tightly controlled media visits."[38] From the resulting media reports, we know that Camp Delta consists of four units. The majority of the inmates are held in three camps described by the government as maximum-security facilities. Inmates are in solitary confinement, restricted to their cells twenty-four hours per day.[39] The inmates are shackled while outside their cells, and they exercise on a "caged 25-foot by 30-foot concrete slab."[40]

The prison currently holds approximately 660 inmates from 42 countries.[41] Though some inmates have been released in the past 18 months, others have replaced them, and for the past year, the prison has maintained approximately the same number of inmates.[42]

LEGAL ANALYSIS: THE BUSH ADMINISTRATION'S POSITION

The U.S. Supreme Court issued decisions in the Padilla and Hamdi cases on June 28, 2004. In order to better understand these decisions, however, we must first take a look at what the government argued in these cases as they wound their way through the courts.

In support of its claim that this new power of indefinite detention had historically been vested in the president, the government
argued that the power was a product of the combined constitutional authority given to Congress to make the laws and the
authority given to the president to enforce the laws as executive
and commander in chief. The government rested its position in significant part upon its interpretation of the Supreme Court's decision in *Ex parte Quirin*, 317 U.S. 1 (1942). The Quirin case arose
during World War II, when eight trained saboteurs who were
members of the German armed forces landed on the shores of
Florida and Long Island, New York, on a mission to destroy war
industries and war facilities within the United States.[43] After their
arrest, President Roosevelt, by means of proclamation and military
order, ordered the eight men to be tried for crimes against the
law of war and violations of the Articles of War before a military
tribunal. One of the eight to be tried, Herbert Hans Haupt, was
a naturalized American citizen.

During the military tribunal, counsel for the German soldiers
challenged the power of the military tribunal to hear their case,
claiming that they were entitled to a jury trial in a civil court.
Noting first that the soldiers, after consultation with counsel, had
admitted that they were unlawful (or enemy) combatants, the
Supreme Court then proceeded to address the boundaries of the
authority of the military tribunal.[44] As Chief Justice Stone plainly
stated, the "question for decision…[is]…whether it is in the power
of the National Government to place petitioners upon trial before
a military commission for the offenses with which they are
charged."[45] Confronted with this question, the Court reached three
conclusions: (1) that the charges against the saboteurs included
offenses that could be tried before a military commission; (2) that
the commission was "lawfully constituted"—that is, that President
Roosevelt was constitutionally authorized to create the commission
in the form that he had chosen; and (3) that the saboteurs were

being held "in lawful custody" for trial before the commission—that is, that the commission had constitutional authority to try the saboteurs even though the civil courts were open at the time.[46]

The *Quirin* decision, then, focused on the constitutionality of relegating admitted unlawful combatants to a military tribunal rather than permitting them to bring their case before a civilian court in the first instance. The decision does not authorize the indefinite detention of unlawful combatants without charge, counsel, or trial. In fact, in the *Quirin* decision, the Court expressly rejected the government's argument that the petitioners "be denied access to the courts because they are enemy aliens who have entered our territory."[47] As a consequence, each soldier was permitted to file his own petition for a writ of habeas corpus. In reviewing these petitions, moreover, the Supreme Court looked carefully at the petitioners' admissions that they were unlawful combatants in order to ensure that each soldier's conduct properly placed him within the jurisdiction of the military tribunal.[48]

In short, *Quirin* does not authorize the president to indefinitely detain citizens without due process. Unable to rely upon the holding of that decision, the government fabricates the construct of "enemy combatant" status and postulates that a single passage in *Quirin* supports its creation:

> Lawful combatants are subject to capture and detention as prisoners of war by opposing military forces. Unlawful combatants are likewise subject to capture and detention, but in addition they are subject to trial and punishment by military tribunals for acts which render their belligerency unlawful.[49]

The government sought to use the phrase "capture and detention" as support for its contention that the executive may imprison citizens indefinitely as "enemy combatants" without trial and without affording them the substantive and procedural rights granted prisoners of war. But the *Quirin* court did not use the term "enemy combatant" to refer to a category of persons who could be detained in this way—wholly without constitutional rights. Rather, the Court used that term to refer to "unlawful combatants" as that category is defined in the law of war.[50] The Court described an "unlawful combatant" as an "enemy combatant who without uniform comes secretly through the lines for the purpose of waging war by destruction of life or property."[51] The *Quirin* court thus used the term "enemy combatant" as a synonym for "unlawful combatant," not as a separately recognized designation.

In reality, the Bush administration has borrowed the term "enemy combatant" from a single reference in *Quirin* and applied it to a newly fabricated category of its own manufacture, with a new set of rules completely untethered from the law of war— rules that permit indefinite detention without notice, charge, hearing, conviction, sentencing, or appeal. Pursuant to the president's "enemy combatant" declaration, then, an American citizen can be stripped of all constitutional rights, detained indefinitely, held incommunicado, and subjected to relentless interrogation unchecked by any of the conventional norms of due process.

Even more disturbing, however, the government has contended that its ability to declare a citizen an "enemy combatant" is a legitimate exercise of its executive discretion that is not subject to judicial review.[52] Under the Bush administration's view, then, no court may inquire into the basis for the president's declaration. On this basis, the government has kept secret how someone may be classified as an "enemy combatant." It has refused to disclose the screening criteria it claims to use to assess what constitutes an "enemy combatant." The government's post hoc recitation of the executive's internal review of the determination cannot compensate in any way for the utter lack of due process afforded Padilla and Hamdi to contest the legality of their detentions in any forum. In this regard, too, the government's reliance on *Quirin* is misplaced. In *Quirin*, unlike here, the Nazi saboteurs were charged with war crimes established *pursuant to statutes enacted by Congress.*[53] There was no presidential declaration without basis in existing law. In sum, neither *Quirin*, nor any other decision of the Supreme Court, provides authority for executive detention of the sort at issue here.[54]

Seizing on a term used by the Court in *Quirin*, the Bush administration has contended that the president's declaration of "enemy combatant" status alone is all that is needed in order for a person to be legally sentenced to indefinite detention without charge or trial. The designation itself, the administration contends, renders entirely superfluous all of the criminal due process protections afforded citizens under the Constitution when they are seized, accused, detained, tried, convicted, and punished. In this regard, the government sought to resurrect the unsuccessful argument advanced by Attorney General James Speed in *Ex parte Milligan*, 71 U.S. (4 Wall.) 2, 14 (1866), that when the country is at war, the president becomes "the supreme legislator, supreme judge, and supreme executive." However, the Constitution does not permit such a rearrangement and concentration of powers and the Supreme Court has never sanctioned one.

THE SUPREME COURT'S DECISIONS IN THE PADILLA AND HAMDI CASES

The Decision in Rumsfeld v. Padilla

In its decision in *Rumsfeld v. Padilla*, Chief Justice Rehnquist, writing the majority opinion for five justices of the Court (Justices Scalia, O'Connor, Kennedy, and Thomas, as well as himself), declined to address the merits of Padilla's claim that he had been unlawfully detained and instead focused on the technical issue of who is the proper party (called a respondent in a habeas case) to be named in a habeas petition. According to the majority, the papers filed on Padilla's behalf should have named Commander Melanie Marr, the commander of the South Carolina naval brig where Padilla is being held, as the respondent, rather than Secretary of Defense Donald Rumsfeld, because she is "the jailer." In support of its decision, the majority noted the Court's "longstanding practice confirm[ing] that in habeas challenges to present physical confinement . . . the default rule is that the proper respondent is the warden of the facility where the prisoner is being held." The effect of this principle, the Court held, was not only that the wrong person had been sued, but that the case had been filed in the wrong federal district. Padilla's petition should have been filed in the federal district in which he was confined. By focusing on this issue, the majority was able to delay by another day its consideration of the real issues in the case: the legality of the president's use of the new "enemy combatant" declaration to hold Padilla without charge or trial or access to counsel. However, the dissenting justices in the case, Justices Stevens, Souter, Ginsburg, and Breyer, were not content with this delay.

Justice Stevens, writing for the dissenters, disagreed with the majority's characterization of the "bright-line" rule regarding naming the warden and filing in the district where the petitioner is being held, and noted that this rule has been "riddled" with exceptions. The more functional approach, Justice Stevens noted, is to focus on the person who has the power to release the prisoner—here, the secretary of defense. After dispensing with the technical grounds for the majority's decision, the dissenting opinion turns to the merits of Padilla's claims, addressing the central issue of whether Padilla "is entitled to a hearing on the justification for his detention." Justice Stevens concluded that Congress's Authorization for Use of Military Force Joint Resolution does not authorize the indefinite, incommunicado detention of

American citizens in the United States. In an impassioned statement, he summed up the outrage of the dissenters:

> At stake in this case is nothing less than the essence of a free society. Even more important than the method of selecting the people's rulers and their successors is the character of the constraints imposed on the Executive by the rule of law. Unconstrained Executive detention for the purpose of investigating and preventing subversive activity is the hallmark of the Star Chamber. Access to counsel for the purpose of protecting the citizen from official mistakes and mistreatment is the hallmark of due process. Executive detention of subversive citizens, like detention of enemy soldiers to keep them off the battlefield, may sometimes be justified to prevent persons from launching or becoming missiles of destruction. It may not, however, be justified by the naked interest in using unlawful procedures to extract information. Incommunicado detention for months on end is such a procedure. Whether the information procured is more or less reliable than that acquired by more extreme forms of torture is of no consequence. For if this Nation is to remain true to the ideals symbolized by its flag, it must not wield the tools of tyrants even to resist an assault by the forces of tyranny.[55]

The dismissal of Padilla's case forced him to begin the case all over again in South Carolina. His lawyer has already done this. The government not only achieved a delay in the resolution of the case, it also succeeded in establishing the principle that it can choose the court in which it litigates by choosing the facility in which to imprison detainees. It seems likely that Padilla will face a tougher court in South Carolina than he did in New York, where his case was originally filed and he was successful on appeal.

The Decision in Hamdi v. Rumsfeld

In *Hamdi v. Rumsfeld*, Justice Sandra Day O'Connor wrote an opinion in which only three other justices joined (Chief Justice Rehnquist, and Justices Kennedy and Breyer), making the decision a "plurality" decision of the Court. The remaining justices had differing responses to the plurality decision.[56]

Addressing the issue discussed by Justice Stevens in his dissent in *Padilla*, Justice O'Connor first concluded that Congress's Authorization for Use of Military Force trumps the existing federal law that provides that no "citizen shall be imprisoned or otherwise detained by the United States except pursuant to an Act of Congress." According to Justice O'Connor, when Congress gave the president the authority to pursue those responsible for the attacks of September 11, that authority must have included the power to detain enemy forces captured in battle. This power, she noted, is consistent with international humanitarian law, which permits a nation to detain enemy forces captured in battle (POWs) until the end of hostilities in order to prevent them from rejoining their forces.

More important, however, Justice O'Connor narrowly defined the category of those who may be detained under this regime. The plurality, then, defines the "enemy combatant" category as those who are "part of or supporting forces hostile to the United States or coalition partners in Afghanistan and who engaged in an armed conflict against the United States there." Justice O'Connor noted further that because the detention is for the purpose of "prevent[ing] a combatant's return to the battlefield," which is "a fundamental incident of waging war," this type of detention is only authorized "for the duration of the particular conflict in which they were captured." In Hamdi's case, the plurality opinion holds; he cannot be held until the end of the "war on terror"—which the plurality acknowledged may not come in Hamdi's lifetime—but only until the end of "active combat operations in Afghanistan." Finally, expressly ruling out the Bush administration's articulated justification for Hamdi's detention (as well as that for Padilla's detention), the plurality stated affirmatively: "Certainly, we agree that indefinite detention for the purpose of interrogation is not authorized."

Having addressed these issues, Justice O'Connor characterized the real question before the Court: not whether Congress has authorized the president to detain "enemy combatants," but rather whether the president's exercise of that power to detain American citizens without serious judicial review violates the Fifth Amendment's rule that no person may be deprived of his liberty without "due process of law." Devising a test that seeks to balance the potentially grave harm resulting from erroneous, indefinite imprisonment of an individual against the burden placed on the military to contend with challenges brought by those seeking judicial review of their detentions, Justice O'Connor stated: "A citizen-detainee seeking to challenge his classification as an enemy-combatant must receive notice of the factual basis of his classification, and a fair opportunity to rebut the Government's factual assertions before a neutral decisionmaker." She noted further that Hamdi "unquestionably has the right to access to counsel in connection" with these proceedings. As Professor Ronald Dworkin noted in his article "What the Court Really Said,"[57] the plurality's balancing test is an effort to walk a tightrope between the district court's opinion that detainees like Hamdi are entitled to all of the constitutional protections afforded criminal defendants—a ruling that the Supreme Court plurality considered too costly in terms of security needs—and the court of appeals' opinion that the president's declaration of "enemy combatant" status could not be challenged at all, a ruling that the plurality thought gave too little protection to the individual being held.

While at first glance these requirements seem to provide citizens with protection should they fall subject to an "enemy combatant" declaration, in reality, the review procedure established by the Court here should offer little comfort to those detained on such grounds. First, according to Justice O'Connor's plurality opinion, the neutral tribunal to which "enemy combatants" must be allowed to appeal to challenge their detention need not be a federal court; rather, the government may establish military commissions to hear these cases. Second, the rules governing what evidence would be acceptable in such hearings are much more favorable to the government than are those rules in a criminal proceeding. The use of hearsay evidence, for example, would be permissible—uncorroborated statements made by people not testifying in court therefore could be the basis for a citizen's continued detention. Finally, and most concerning, is Justice O'Connor's statement that the Constitution would permit the government to create a presumption in its favor, so that the detainee would be compelled to prove that he is not an "enemy combatant" and thus establish his innocence. By turning the foundational principle of our criminal justice system on its head, the plurality has built a mountain that few detainees could ever successfully climb.

AN IN-DEPTH CRITIQUE OF THE DECISIONS

The presidential declarations that Jose Padilla and Yaser Hamdi are "enemy combatants" who may be detained indefinitely for the duration of the government's "war on terrorism" are an attack not only on our most basic right of individual liberty, but also on one of the fundamental premises of our constitutional democracy: the separation of powers principle. This attack by the executive branch has several faces, each of which engenders serious cause for concern.

The first, and overarching, issue involves the president's unlawful use of the commander in chief power to address domestic affairs. Constitutional text, structure, doctrine, and theory make plain the severe limitations placed on the executive's exercise of war powers within the United States.

The second issue involves the government's twofold presumption that the power to create an undefined category of individuals who may be detained indefinitely for investigatory reasons *exists*, and that this power resides *exclusively* in the executive branch. There is, however, no constitutional, common law, or statutory basis for such an arrogation of power or its unfettered exercise. Indeed, the executive's use of its newly "found" power fatally undermines the rule of law by running roughshod over Congress's prior enactments expressly intended to curtail the use of Executive detention and its recent pronouncements about the proper scope of the war powers to be exercised in the wake of the September 11 attacks.

Third, the presidential declaration that Padilla, Hamdi, and others may be indefinitely detained as "enemy combatants" violates fundamental due process requirements. The lack of any definition of this category or its constituent offenses, and the absence of any rules circumscribing the exercise of discretion and limiting the potential for arbitrary enforcement, constitute an egregious violation of our most basic due process principles. In addition, the government's argument—first articulated in the *Hamdi* case and subsequently reiterated in a softer tone in the *Padilla* case—amounts to a contention that persons denoted "enemy combatants" are not entitled to meaningful habeas corpus review. In this regard, the government's position violates the Suspension Clause of the Constitution, which requires the availability of habeas corpus relief for those detained by executive action, and violates the Due Process Clause because it denies individuals a federal forum in which to challenge a substantial deprivation of liberty.

THE SEPARATION OF POWERS DOCTRINE PRECLUDES THE PRESIDENT FROM USING HIS COMMANDER IN CHIEF POWERS DOMESTICALLY ABSENT EXPRESS CONGRESSIONAL AUTHORIZATION

The separation of powers principle was designed in support of a fundamental insight of the Framers: that the concentration of power in the hands of a single branch is a threat to liberty. From the very beginning of our republic, this axiom was articulated in the most explicit terms: "The accumulation of all powers, Legislative, Executive, and Judiciary, in the same hands . . . may justly be pronounced the very definition of tyranny."[58] Quoting Montesquieu, the Federalists stressed the point that liberty, in the fundamental political sense of the term, demands limits on the ability of one branch to influence political decisions:

> When the legislative and executive powers are united in the same person or body, there can be no liberty, because apprehensions may arise lest the same monarch or senate should enact tyrannical laws to execute them in a tyrannical manner. Were the power of judging joined with the legislative, the life and liberty of the subject would be exposed to arbitrary control for the judge would then be the legislator. Were it joined to the executive power, the judge might behave with all the violence of an oppressor.[59]

The structure of separation of powers protects our core constitutional values by providing three separate, overlapping, and mutually reinforcing remedies—legislative, executive, and judicial—against unconstitutional federal conduct. By increasing the power of the president beyond what the Framers envisioned, the executive's new "enemy combatant" policy compromises the liberty of this country's citizens, "liberty which the separation of powers seeks to secure."[60]

Such an expansion of presidential power is unconstitutional for two reasons. First, while the executive has power to conduct military operations abroad, he cannot unilaterally expand this power to intrude upon domestic affairs inside the borders of the country and detain U.S. citizens without charge or trial. Second, the president's aggrandizement of his military powers as commander in chief encroaches upon the constitutional authority of Congress and the Courts over domestic affairs.

THE DISCRETION ACCORDED THE PRESIDENT'S CONDUCT OF MILITARY OPERATIONS ABROAD IS NOT ACCORDED TO HIS ACTIONS ADDRESSING DOMESTIC AFFAIRS, EVEN DURING WARTIME

The Supreme Court has long recognized that the distinction between internal and external governmental affairs is a critical factor that must be assessed when a court examines the scope of constitutional authority accorded a specific branch of government, and, in particular, when it assesses the executive branch's exercise of its war powers.[61] Justice Jackson's argument—made in *Youngstown Sheet & Tube Co. v. Sawyer*, 343 U.S. 579, 645 (1952), the case challenging President Truman's attempted seizure of the country's steel mills during the Korean War—is relevant to our circumstances now: the distinction between congressionally unauthorized presidential actions directed at extraterritorial activity and similar presidential actions focused on the "internal affairs of the country" is critical.[62]

The principle is well established that significant deference is given to the president's authority as commander in chief to act in external affairs, even in the absence of an express congressional grant of authority.[63] Yet, *until now*, the Supreme Court has never accepted the proposition that the president's commander-in-chief authority, standing alone, may be turned inward to intrude upon domestic affairs, even in times of national security threats or undeclared wars.[64]

The president's military powers were never intended "to supercede representative government of internal affairs," a proposition that Justice Jackson found "obvious from the Constitution and from elementary American history."[65] In this regard, Justice Jackson declared in *Youngstown* that "no doctrine that the Court could promulgate would seem to me more sinister and alarming than that a president whose conduct of foreign affairs is so largely uncontrolled, and often even is unknown, can vastly enlarge his mastery over the internal affairs of the country by his own commitment of the Nation's armed force to some foreign venture."[66]

Constitutional text, structure, doctrine, and theory recognize that Congress, and not the president, holds the authority to permit the imposition of military power within the domestic arena. When the Framers drafted the Constitution, they weakened the possibility of a military with a dominant role in American society by subordinating it to civilian control both by appointing the president as its civilian head, and, more significantly, by authorizing the other two branches of the government to exercise control over the armed forces. Of those branches, Congress has the most practical and determinative authority to exercise influence over the military.[67] As Justice Jackson concluded in *Youngstown*, even the specter of war does not detract from this constitutional principle:

> Thus, even in war time [the president's] seizure of needed military housing [within the United States] must be authorized by Congress. It was also left expressly to Congress to "provide for calling forth the

Militia to execute the Laws of the Union, suppress insurrections and repel Invasions...." Such a limitation on the command power, written at a time when the militia rather than a standing army was contemplated as the military weapon of the Republic, underscores the Constitution's policy that Congress, not the Executive, should control utilization of the war power as an instrument of domestic policy.[68]

The *Youngstown* opinions are all the more relevant today considering that these limitations on the internal use of the commander in chief power was affirmed in the face of the global threat to security created by the Korean War—concerns about which were as serious then as are our present-day concerns about global terrorism.[69]

The president has only constitutionally exercised his commander in chief power within the United States in the few limited circumstances when Congress has passed a law permitting the internal use of military authority. In these few cases, the Supreme Court acknowledged that the commander in chief power had been expressly augmented by a grant of congressional authority. In no case has the Court viewed these exercises of power as an inherent war power—that is, as a part of the president's inherent commander in chief authority. Without this congressional authorization, however, the exercise of commander in chief powers in domestic affairs is an unconstitutional aggrandizement of the executive's power. As discussed below, further constitutional concerns are raised by the nature of this aggrandizement, which encroaches upon the authority of Congress and the Courts over domestic affairs.

There is no statute that expressly authorizes the President to detain individuals without due process indefinitely merely upon his designation that they are "enemy combatants"; there is no act of Congress from which this power may be properly implied;[70] and there is no constitutional well from which the President can draw this prerogative.[71] In fact, to the contrary, both Congress and the courts have acted emphatically to limit the executive's power to detain American citizens without review under circumstances like those present here.[72]

THE TEXT AND LEGISLATIVE HISTORY OF THE ANTIDETENTION STATUTE REQUIRES SPECIFIC STATUTORY AUTHORIZATION FOR THE DETENTION OF CITIZENS

Congress has not "left open" any issue concerning the legality of detaining U.S. citizens without charge or trial, regardless of whether the United States is at war or involved in a military conflict abroad;[73] it has expressly prohibited this type of investigative/preventative detention through its enactment of the anti-detention statute.

Congress's antidetention statute, 18 U.S.C. § 4001(a), provides that "no citizen shall be imprisoned or otherwise detained by the United States except pursuant to an Act of Congress." The text is unambiguous, permitting no exceptions to its proscription of executive detentions that have not been specifically authorized by statute.

The legislative history of § 4001(a) makes clear that Congress intended to deprive the executive of the power to detain American citizens during *wartime* unless it has given the president an explicit statutory authorization. The antidetention statute was enacted specifically to ensure that wartime detentions of American citizens without due process—like the internments of Japanese-Americans during World War II—do not happen again. Congressman Tom Railsback, who introduced the provision now codified as 18 U.S.C. § 4001(a), stated that the express purpose of the provision was "to try to do something about what occurred in 1942 through President Roosevelt's Executive Order."[74] Railsback emphasized that the Judiciary Committee wanted to "do something affirmative ... to make sure that we have restricted the President's *wartime* powers."[75]

The House Report indicates that the "purpose of the ... bill" was, as an initial matter, "to repeal the Emergency Detention Act of 1950 ... which both authorizes the establishment of detention camps and imposes certain conditions on their use."[76] The Emergency Detention Act had authorized the U.S. attorney general, during internal security emergencies, to apprehend and detain "each person as to whom there is reasonable cause to believe that such person probably will engage in, or probably will conspire with others to engage in, acts of espionage or of sabotage."[77]

The House Report on § 4001(a) stated that the "mere continued existence" of the Emergency Detention Act had "aroused much concern among American citizens, lest the Detention Act become an instrumentality for apprehending and detaining citizens who hold unpopular beliefs and views."[78] But § 4001(a) was intended to be more than a negation of the Emergency Detention Act:

> [I]t is not enough to merely repeal the Detention Act. The Act concededly can be viewed as not merely an authorization but in some respects as a restriction on detention. Repeal alone might leave citizens subject to arbitrary executive action, with no clear demarcation of the limits of executive authority. It has been suggested that repeal alone would leave us where we were prior to 1950. The Committee believes that imprisonment or other detention of citizens should be limited to situations in which a statutory authorization, an Act of Congress, exists.[79]

Congress was concerned that merely repealing the Emergency Detention Act might allow courts to infer that some executive detention powers over citizens would remain when the next wartime crisis arose. The intent of Congress in passing § 4001(a), and of President Nixon in signing it, was to ensure that if a future president sought to invoke wartime preventative detention powers, the courts would analyze them under the "severe test" of Justice Jackson's third category (explicit congressional disapproval) and foreclose application of all executive detention powers.

Obviously, with § 4001(a), Congress expressed a clear public policy against the detention of citizens, in wartime or at peace, even for citizens "likely to engage in espionage or sabotage."[80] Congress did so in a time of war, with widespread domestic dissent focused on that war, and in a climate of major political assassinations and even domestic terrorism. The Supreme Court, in a prior case addressing the applicability of the statute, has declared that "the plain language of § 4001(a) prescribes detention *of any kind* by the United States, absent a congressional grant of authority to detain."[81] Nothing in the legislative history, the text, or the text's subsequent construction by courts indicates that the clear proscription of § 4001(a) should be ignored here.

THE PRESIDENT'S DESIGNATION AND DETENTION OF U.S. CITIZENS AS "ENEMY COMBATANTS" IS AN UNCONSTITUTIONAL ENCROACHMENT UPON CONGRESS'S AUTHORITY

The president here deliberately sought to unilaterally expand his commander in chief power, not only in the absence of express congressional authorization but in the face of incompatible congressional acts.

It is beyond question that Congress has the constitutional power to regulate the detention of American citizens who are captured within the United States during time of war or military conflict. The

Constitution does not limit Congress's war powers to the authorization or declaration of war; rather, it explicitly provides Congress with a panoply of war powers, including (1) the power to "make Rules concerning Captures on Land and Water,"[82] (2) the sole authority to authorize the seizure of citizens' homes for military purposes during times of war (U.S. Const. amend. III); and (3) the exclusive power to authorize the seizure of enemy property within the United States during wartime.[83] If Congress has the authority to limit the president's commander in chief power to capture ships on the high seas during a time of military conflict, it certainly must have the constitutional authority to limit the president's power to detain American citizens in the United States during wartime.

THE EXECUTIVE'S "ENEMY COMBATANT" POLICY USURPS CONGRESS'S LAWMAKING AUTHORITY

The president's "enemy combatant" policy also impermissibly disrupts the balance of powers between the legislative and executive branches by usurping Congress's legislative power. Article I, section 1 of the Constitution vests in Congress the power to make laws.[84] The executive power, by contrast, is to "Take Care that the Laws be faithfully executed."[85] Congress may not delegate its inherent lawmaking power to another branch, and no other branch may assert this power.[86]

Because the president lacked congressional authorization for his enemy combatant declarations generally, and his June 9, 2002, order regarding Padilla specifically, these orders constitute executive lawmaking.[87] Indeed, the declaration highlights the problems that arise when the president engages in lawmaking under the guise of exercising his commander in chief power. Without clear standards and limits emerging from a congressionally defined authorization to detain U.S. citizens, there is no official articulation of what constitutes an "enemy combatant," what circumstances will trigger the president's designation, and when the detention of a citizen shall cease.

The unfettered and undefined nature of the power the president seeks points to an unconstitutional effort to usurp Congress's authority to define violations of domestic law as well as violations of the Law of Nations. The president's unconstitutional seizure of citizens, no less than the seizure of steel, through executive lawmaking, bypasses constitutional limits upon executive power:

> The Executive, except for recommendation and veto, has no legislative power. The executive action we have here originates in the individual will of the President and represents an exercise of authority without law. No one, perhaps not even the President, knows the limits of the power he may seek to exert in this instance and the parties affected cannot learn the limits of their rights.[88]

The Constitution requires that both the amendment and the repeal of statutes also conform with Article I requirements of bicameral passage and presentment to the president.[89] The president violated these Article I requirements when he acted to effectively cancel 18 U.S.C. § 4001(a), a statute duly enacted by Congress that expressly prohibited the type of detention at issue here. A law can only be repealed or amended through another independent legislative enactment, which itself must conform with the requirements of Article I. The president's policy thus violates Article I's "single, finely wrought and exhaustively considered procedure,"[90] and is therefore unconstitutional on these grounds as well.

THE EXECUTIVE'S VIEW OF THE SCOPE OF JUDICIAL REVIEW IMPROPERLY EXPROPRIATES CONGRESS'S SUSPENSION CLAUSE POWER

The Constitution explicitly guarantees the legislative branch a role in any curtailment of habeas corpus. "The Privilege of the Writ of Habeas Corpus shall not be suspended, unless when in Cases of Rebellion or Invasion the public Safety may require it."[91] Courts have consistently refused to recognize executive discretion to add further exceptions to the constitutional text. During the early days of the Civil War, Chief Justice Taney stated that neither the president's officers nor the president himself could suspend the writ, and that no exception could be made "in any emergency or in any state of things."[92] By denying Padilla access to counsel and the opportunity to challenge the government's evidence, and by urging the court to apply the "some evidence" standard, which forecloses meaningful review of the jurisdictional facts underlying his "enemy combatant" status, the government has effectively suspended the writ of habeas corpus and trenched on Congress's exclusive power in this field.

CONCLUSION

The Bush administration has created and used its "enemy combatant" classification as a permanent legal category, not limited by the scope of the hostilities or the scope of the congressional authorization to use force, and not constrained in any way by the requirements of domestic constitutional law or international humanitarian law. It has been widely reported that the Department of Defense is considering creating long-term detention camps at Guantánamo for "enemy combatants."[93] These reports should evoke memories of *Korematsu*—the case challenging the unlawful and immoral detention of Japanese-Americans during World War II—if for no other reason than to show us in the starkest possible terms what a devastating precedent these cases could become. These "enemy combatant" camps may become a permanent feature of our legal landscape. Is this what we want to be known and remembered for?

By taking away the most significant constitutional rights incident to citizenship, the "enemy combatant" designation effectively strips people of their birth citizenship without charge or trial—a power that the Fourteenth Amendment denies to any branch of government.[94] This new category of "enemy combatant" has the potential to circumvent the Constitution's heightened procedural protections for citizens accused of treason,[95] protections that were included in the Constitution to counter abuses by which the executive, through amorphous sedition laws, has historically punished political dissent.[96] And while the Supreme Court has stated that "[c]itizenship *is* man's basic right for it is nothing less than the right to have rights,"[97] in today's world the Geneva Conventions and international law convey certain rights irrespective of citizenship. The government has negated all of these rights by invoking the phrase "enemy combatant" without providing a definition for the status or an adequate explanation of why it applies to Mr. Padilla or Mr. Hamdi or the detainees in Guantánamo.

When our executive's action broadcasts such a wanton disregard for the laws of this country and for the international community, we must look to the other branches of government to ensure that the country continues down the road originally taken by the founders toward justice, not away from it. And if those we have placed in office do not respond to our call for executive obedience to the morals and values embedded in our Constitution, then we must use the power of the people to make that happen.

NOTES

1   International humanitarian law is a branch of public international law that seeks to circumscribe the boundaries of armed conflicts and reduce the suffering that they cause in the world. This branch of international law is based on the notion that the methods and means of warfare are subject to ethical and legal limitations, and that the victims of armed conflict are entitled to humanitarian care and protection. International humanitarian law constitutes one of the two branches of the laws of armed conflict, and is termed the *jus in bello* (the law in war). The other branch is known as the *jus ad bellum* (the law to war).

2   *Ex parte Quirin*, 317 U.S. 1 (1942).

3   *Quirin*, 317 U.S. at 27–36; Additional Protocol I, art. 43(2).

4   *Quirin*, 317 U.S. at 31.

5   The Geneva Conventions consist of four international law instruments: the Geneva Convention for the Amelioration of the Condition of the Wounded and Sick in Armed Forces in the Field, Aug. 12, 1949, 6 U.S.T. 3114, 75 U.N.T.S. 31; the Geneva Convention for the Amelioration of the Condition of the Wounded, Sick and Shipwrecked Members of Armed Forces at Sea, Aug. 12, 1949, 6 U.S.T. 3217, 75 U.N.T.S. 85; the Geneva Convention Relative to the Treatment of Prisoners of War, Aug. 12, 1949, 6 U.S.T. 3316, 75 U.N.T.S. 135; and the Geneva Convention Relative to the Protection of Civilian Persons in Time of War, Aug. 12, 1949, 6 U.S.T. 3516, 75 U.N.T.S. 287. Article 2, common to all four Conventions, provides that "the present Convention shall apply to all cases of declared war or of any other armed conflict which may arise between two or more of the High Contracting parties, even if the state of war is not recognized by one of them."

6   Article 13 of the Third Geneva Convention delineates the basic standard of treatment for POWs indicating that they "must at all times be humanely treated." Geneva Convention III, art. 13, 75 U.N.T.S. at 146. Specifically, they must not be unlawfully killed or endangered, physically mutilated, or subjected to medical or scientific experiment. Article 13 also requires that POWs be protected from violence, intimidation, insults, and public curiosity. Article 15 requires that POWs receive the proper medical attention that their state of health requires. Art. 15, 75 U.N.T.S. at 148. Article 17 states that POWs may not be coerced into supplying information to the capturing power; they are only bound to supply their name, rank, and number. Art. 17, 75 U.N.T.S. at 150. Article 21 provides that prisoners may not be held in close confinement except when necessary to safeguard their health, and Article 22 requires that they not be interned in unhealthy areas or where the climate is injurious to them. Art 21, 75 U.N.T.S. at 152–54; art. 22, 75 U.N.T.S. at 154. Articles 22–38 mandate the provision of sufficient quantity of food rations of quality and variety to prevent weight loss and the development of nutritional deficiencies, the provision of regular medical attention, the opportunity for physical exercise and for the practice of their religion.

7   *See* Third Geneva Convention, art. 5, 6 U.S.T. at 3322–24, 75 U.N.T.S. at 140–42.

8   U.S. Const. art. VI, cl. 2.

9   *See* Army Regulation 190-8, Enemy Prisoners of War, Retained Personnel, Civilian Internees and Other Detainees § 1-5(a)(2) (1997) (available at

http://www.apd.army.mil/pdffiles/r190_8.pdf, March 26, 2004). Army Regulation 190-8 (hereafter "AR 190-8") states:

> In accordance with Article 5 [Third Geneva Convention], if any doubt arises
> as to whether a person, having committed a belligerent act and been taken
> into custody by U.S. Armed Forces, belongs to any of the categories enu-
> merated in Article 4 [Third Geneva Convention], such persons shall enjoy
> the protection of the present Convention until such time as their status has
> been determined by a competent tribunal.

AR 190-8 § 1-6(a) (1997).

10 *See* AR 190-8, §§ 1-6(c), (e).

11 The internal secret procedure for determining who may be designated an "enemy combatant" was recited for the first time in the government's Supreme Court brief. This procedure plainly does not comport with any notion of due process, whether that notion is
anchored in our domestic jurisprudence or in the law of war. At a minimum, the drafters
of Article 5 made clear that the competent tribunal requirement ensures that "decisions
which might have the gravest consequences [would] not be left to a single person." Jean
de Preux et al., Geneva Convention Relative to the Treatment of Prisoners of War:
Commentary 77 (1960).

12 *See* Government's Supreme Court Brief in *Rumsfeld, Secretary of Defense v. Padilla, et al.,*
No. 03-1027 at 9.

13 *See* presidential declaration of June 9, 2002, filed in Civil Action No. 02-CV-0445
(MBM).

14 *See* Mobbs Declaration, dated September 30, 2002, filed in Civil Action No. 02-CV-0445
(MBM).

15 Ibid.

16 Ibid.

17 *See* Jacoby Declaration, dated January 9, 2003, submitted in Civil Action No. 02-CV-
0445 (MBM).

18 Ibid.

19 Ibid.

20 These are the facts as they have been alleged in the habeas corpus petition—the procedural petition demanding that jailers justify in court their detention of a person—filed
on Hamdi's behalf by his father and his attorneys.

21 *See* Government's Supreme Court Brief in *Hamdi et al. v. Rumsfeld, Secretary of Defense, et
al.,* No. 03-6696 at 4.

22 Government's Supreme Court Brief in *Hamdi et al. v. Rumsfeld, Secretary of Defense, et al.,*
No. 03-6696 at 5.

23 *See* Government's Supreme Court Brief in *Hamdi et al. v. Rumsfeld, Secretary of Defense, et
al.,* No. 03-6696 at 6-7.

24 Reports of interviews of Hamdi were deemed exculpatory by United States District
Judge Ellis in *United States v. John Phillip Walker Lindh,* Crim. No. 02-37-A (E.D.\Va.,
Alexandria Division, 2001) on the issue of whether Lindh was an "enemy combatant."
These interview reports are nonclassified, and were turned over to counsel for Lindh in

that case, who have said that it is not unreasonable to infer that Hamdi's statements are exculpatory to him as well on the enemy combatant issue.

25   67 *Fed. Reg.* 35596 (May 20, 2002).

26   The district court observed that "[t]he declaration is silent as to what level of 'affiliation' is necessary to warrant enemy combatant status."

27   The government places great emphasis on the fact that Hamdi was armed in reaching its conclusion that there is sufficient evidence to establish that he was an enemy combatant. However, because carrying a weapon in Afghanistan is commonplace, it does not support an inference that one is a combatant. People in Afghanistan even take weapons to weddings and fire celebratory shots in the air. Eric Schmitt, "U.S. Describes Ground Fire From Afghan Wedding," *New York Times*, July 4, 2002, A6. The *Washington Post* described this as "the traditional, exuberant spraying of rifle fire in the air." Pamela Constable, "Before Attack, 'We Never Heard the Sound of the Planes,'" *Washington Post*, July 4, 2002, A16.

28   *See* Government's Supreme Court Brief in *Hamdi et al. v. Rumsfeld, Secretary of Defense, et al.*, No. 03-6696 at 4.

29   Joint Appendix, submitted in *Hamdi et al. v. Rumsfeld, Secretary of Defense, et al.*, No. 03-6696, at 148-150.

30   Ibid.

31   Although the Mobbs Declaration is silent on this point, the government suggests that Taliban detainees are "unlawful combatants" based on a presidential determination that all Taliban detainees are unlawful combatants. The government, however, says that the Supreme Court need not address the issue of whether Hamdi is an unlawful combatant. As noted above, under the Third Geneva Convention, 6 U.S.T. 3316, 75 U.N.T.S. 135, and under current United States military regulations, such determinations must be made on an individual basis by a competent tribunal. Because the government's detention is punitive (e.g., jail-type institution that houses criminals; solitary confinement separated from all other members of his unit), Hamdi is being treated as an unlawful combatant without first having a competent tribunal determine that status. Therefore, his current detention is unlawful.

32   Under Mr. Lindh's plea agreement, in exchange for Mr. Lindh's ongoing cooperation with government investigations, the government expressly agrees to "forego any right it has to treat [Mr. Lindh] as an unlawful enemy combatant." Plea Agreement, *United States v. Lindh* (E.D.Va. 2002) (No. 02-37-A), ¶21.

33   The administration has to date been unwilling or unable to explain how it decides whether someone is an enemy combatant and can be held without charge, or a criminal subject to federal law. According to a report in the *New York Law Journal*, "Walking a Thin Line," published on November 22, 2002:

> When asked how an enemy combatant designation is made, the White House referred the question to the Justice Department. The Justice Department referred the question to the White House. The White House did not return subsequent phone inquiries.

Available at: http://www.nylawyer.com/news/02/11/112202h.html.

34 The British and Australian governments have confirmed some of the detainees who are incarcerated on the base.

35 *Rasul et al. v. Bush, President of the United States, et al.*, Nos. 03-334 and 03-343.

36 *See* Regulations Respecting the Laws and Customs of War on Land, art. 1, annex to Convention (No. IV) Respecting the Laws and Customs of War on Land, Oct. 18, 1907, 36 Stat. 2277, 1 Bevans 631; Geneva Convention III, art. 4; Protocol Additional to the Geneva Conventions of 12 August 1949, and Relating to the Protection of Victims of International Armed Conflicts, opened for signature Dec. 12, 1977, arts. 43, 44, 1125 U.N.T.S. 3.

37 Katharine Q. Seelye, "A Nation Challenged: Captives; An Uneasy Routine at Cuba Prison Camp," *New York Times*, March 16, 2002 (quoting Deputy Commander at Guantánamo).

38 Charles Savage, "For Detainees At Guantánamo, Daily Benefits—and Uncertainty," *Miami Herald,* August 24, 2003.

39 Ibid.

40 Ibid.

41 "Suspect at Guantánamo Attempts Suicide," Associated Press, August 26, 2003.

42 *See, e.g.,* "Tales of Despair from Guantánamo," *New York Times*, June 17, 2003.

43 *Exparte Quirin*, 317 U.S 1 (1946) at 20–21.

44 Ibid. at 20–21, 46.

45 Ibid. at 29.

46 The fact that the *Quirin* court determined that a military tribunal may, in certain cases, provide constitutionally adequate process for unlawful combatants charged with violations of the law of war does not mean that military tribunals are necessarily appropriate for all those properly determined to be unlawful combatants. As the Supreme Court acknowledged in *Quirin*: "There are some acts regarded . . . as offenses against the law of war which would *not* be triable by military tribunal here, either because they are not recognized by our courts as violations of the law of war or because they are of that class of offenses constitutionally triable only by a jury." *Quirin,* 317 U.S. at 29 (emphasis added).

47 The government claimed the petitioners "must be denied access to the courts, both because they are enemy aliens or have entered our territory as enemy belligerents, and because the President's Proclamation undertakes in terms to deny such access to the class of persons defined by the Proclamation." *Quirin*, 317 U.S. at 24–25. The Court emphatically rejected the government's construction: "[N]either the Proclamation nor the fact that they are enemy aliens forecloses consideration by the courts of petitioners' contentions that the Constitution and laws of the United States constitutionally enacted forbid their trial by military commission." Ibid. at 24–25.

48 Ibid.

49 *Quirin*, 317 U.S. at 31 (emphasis added).

50 *See Quirin*, 317 U.S. at 30–31 ("By universal agreement and practice the law of war draws a distinction . . . between those who are lawful and unlawful combatants"). "Combatants" are "members of the armed forces of a Party to a conflict," Additional Protocol I, art. 43(2), who fight openly for one side, and who are entitled, upon capture, to prisoner of war status. *Quirin*, 317 U.S. at 27–36. The term "unlawful combatants" includes two sets of people: (1) members of the regular armed forces who do not wear uniforms and do not bear

arms openly, and therefore have lost their privileged combatant status; and (2) civilians who unlawfully participate directly in battle and have never had privileged combatant status from the outset. Ibid. at 31.

51 *Quirin,* 317 U.S. at 31.

52 *Hamdi v. Rumsfeld,* 296 F.3d 278, 283 (4th Cir. 2002). ("The government asserts that 'given the constitutionally limited role of the courts in reviewing military decisions, courts may not second guess the military's determination that an individual is an enemy combatant and may be detained as such.'")

53 Thus, the Court in *Quirin* found it unnecessary to decide the issue of whether the executive has the constitutional power to create military commissions without the support of congressional legislation. *Quirin* 317 U.S. at 29. *See Quirin,* 317 U.S. at 27 ("Articles 81 and 82 [of the Congressionally enacted Articles of War, 10 U.S.C. §§ 1471–1593] authorize trial, either by court martial or military commission, of those charged with relieving, harboring or corresponding with the enemy and those charged with spying."); *Quirin* 317 U.S. at 28–30.("For here *Congress has authorized* trial of offenses against the law of war. . . . It is no objection that *Congress* in providing for the trial of such offenses has not itself undertaken to . . . enumerate or define by statute all the acts which that law condemns. . . . *Congress* had the choice of crystallizing in permanent form and in minute detail every offense against the law of war, or of adopting the system of common law [emphasis mine]. . . .") *See also Madsen v. Kinsella,* 343 U.S. 341, 355 n.22 (1952). (Describing *Quirin* as a case in which the "conviction of saboteurs . . . was upheld on charges of violating the law of war *as defined by statute* [emphasis mine].")

54 The government's reliance on two cases, *Colepaugh v. Looney,* 235 F.2d 429 (10th Cir. 1956), and *In re Territo,* 156 F.2d 142 (9th Cir. 1946), to support its claim to this new power, is similarly misplaced. *Colepaugh,* like *Quirin,* involved the question of whether a military commission had jurisdiction to try the petitioner for specific violations of the law of war, including entering the United States in civilian dress for the purpose of committing espionage. 235 F.2d at 431. The issue of whether the petitioner could have been detained without *any* trial was not addressed. *Territo* has a similar deficiency. That decision too contains no suggestion that the government can detain belligerents without charges or trial. Territo, an American-born Italian army private, was captured in Italy by the United States military during World War II. In reviewing the legality of Mr. Territo's detention by the United States as a prisoner of war, the court reviewed as well the factual basis of his internment.

55 *See* the Supreme Court decision in *Rumsfeld, Secretary of Defense v. Padilla, et al.,* No. 03-1027, 542 U.S. (U.S. June 28, 2004) (Stevens, J., dissenting).

56 Of particular note was the alliance of Justice Stevens, one of the Court's most liberal justices, with Justice Scalia, one of the Court's most conservative justices. The two together argued in their dissent that liberty interest protected by due process does not permit the creation of special regimes to address circumstances like those of Hamdi. In their view, the Court should have ordered that Hamdi be indicted and tried by a criminal court in the normal fashion or released. Justice Thomas, on the other end of this continuum, stated in his dissent that the president as commander-in-chief must have absolute power over

the pursuit of military objectives once congress has authorized that action, and that no court may review the president's decisions in that regard.

57 *New York Review of Books*, 51, No. 13, August 12, 2004.

58 C. Rossiter ed, *The Federalist Papers* (New York: New American Library, 1961), No. 47, 301.

59 *Id.*, No. 47, 303.

60 *Clinton v. New York City*, 524 U.S. 417, 452 (1998) (Kennedy, J., concurring).

61 *See, e.g., United States v. Curtis-Wright Export Corp.*, 299 U.S. 304, 315 (1936). ("That there are differences between [external and internal affairs], and that these differences are fundamental, may not be doubted.") *See also Youngstown Sheet & Tube Co. v. Sawyer*, 343 U.S. 579, 645 (1952) (Jackson, J., concurring). ("I should indulge the widest latitude of interpretation to sustain [the President's] exclusive function to command the instruments of national force, at least when turned against the outside world for the security of our society. But, when it is turned inward . . . it should have no such indulgence.")

62 Hon. Juan R. Torruella, United States Court of Appeals for the First Circuit, *On the Slippery Slope of Afghanistan: Military Commissions and the Exercise of Presidential Power*, 4 U. Pa. J. Const. L. 648, 660–61 (2002).

63 *See, e.g., Youngstown*, 343 U.S. at 635–36 n.2 (Jackson, J., concurring).

64 *See Youngstown*, 343 U.S. at 642 (Jackson, J., concurring); *see also* ibid. at 632 (Douglas, J., concurring). ("[O]ur history and tradition rebel at the thought that the grant of military power carries with it authority over civilian affairs.") *See also Goldwater v. Carter*, 444 U.S. 996, 1004 (1979) (Rehnquist, J., concurring) (reasoning that "in Youngstown, private litigants brought a suit contesting the President's authority under his war powers to seize the Nation's steel industry, an action of profound and demonstrable domestic impact," and that in Curtis-Wright, the effect of the President's action was "entirely external to the United States and [falls] within the category of foreign affairs").

The Supreme Court has cited only two potential circumstances in which the president might exercise his commander-in-chief powers internally absent congressional authorization, neither of which is present in this case: (1) defending against an invasion by a foreign nation or, (2) defending against states organized in rebellion. *See The Prize Cases*, 67 U.S. (2 Black) 635, 668 (1862). The Court has not had occasion to squarely decide the question of the constitutionality of the President's internal exercise of his commander-in-chief authority absent congressional authorization. *See, e.g.,* ibid. at 671. ("Without admitting that such [a congressional] act was necessary under the circumstances, it is plain that if the President had in any manner assumed powers which it was necessary should have the authority or sanction of Congress, that on the well known principle of law, 'omnis ratihabitio retrotrahitur et mandato equiparatur,' this ratification has operated to perfectly cure the defect.") The President's use of military authority within the United States has historically received either prior authorization or subsequent ratification by Congress.

65 *Youngstown*, 343 U.S. at 644 (Jackson, J., concurring*). See also Brown v. United States*, 12 U.S. (8 Cranch) 110 (1814) (holding that the president could not seize, as enemy property, material found on U.S. land at the commencement of hostilities in 1812 without congressional authority); *Fleming v. Page*, 50 U.S. (9 How.) 603 (1850) (finding that the president, as commander-in-chief, could not annex territory to the United States by virtue of a mil-

itary conquest unless he received authority from Congress); *Ex parte Milligan*, 71 U.S. 2 (4 Wall.) 121 (1866). (Military commissions cannot be justified "on the mandate of the President; because he is controlled by law, and has his appropriate sphere of duty, which is to execute, not to make, the laws; and there is no unwritten criminal code to which resort can be had as a source of jurisdiction.")

66 Ibid. at 642.

67 Thus, the Framers gave Congress, not the president, the authority to declare war. United States Constitution art. I, § 8, cl. 11. Congress also has the authority to raise and support an army, ibid. at cl. 12, and a navy, ibid. at cl. 13. Congress may make rules and regulations for the military, ibid. at cl. 14, and call forth the militia, ibid. at cl. 15. Congress must provide advice and consent to the president's appointment of officers, ibid. at art. II, § 2, cl. 2. Perhaps most significant is the constitutional requirement that Congress "raise and support Armies, but no Appropriation of Money to that use shall be for a longer Term than two Years," ibid. at art. I, § 8. This limitation on long-term military funding ensures that Congress maintains an active, regular role in regulating the affairs of the military.

68 Ibid. at 644 (Jackson, J., concurring).

69 *See* ibid. at 668 (Vinson, C.J., dissenting). (Describing the circumstances surrounding the case as follows: "A world not yet recovered from the devastation of World War II has been forced to face the threat of another and more terrifying global conflict.")

70 The plurality's decision that Congress's use of force authorization trumped Congress's anti-detention statute is not well supported by the law or the legislative history. *See, infra*.

71 *See Youngstown*, 343 U.S. at 586–88.

72 *See, e.g.,* 18 U.S.C. § 4001(a) (2001); *Ex Parte Milligan*, 71 U.S. (4 Wall.) 2, 114–16 (1866); *Duncan v. Kahanamoku*, 327 U.S. 304, 323–24 (1946); *Reid v. Covert*, 35 U.S. 1, 17 (1957).

73 Congress has granted the specific authority to the executive it thought necessary and appropriate to enable it to address security threats from abroad. It criminalized specific terrorism-related conduct through the enactment of numerous statutes. *See, e.g.,* 18 U.S.C. § 2332(b) (conspiracy to kill United States nationals); 18 U.S.C. § 844 (bombing and bombing conspiracy); 18 U.S.C. § 2332a(a)(1) (conspiracy to use weapons of mass destruction); 18 U.S.C. § 2441 (defining war crimes). It also considerably broadened the executive branch's law enforcement powers to permit greater surveillance and monitoring of suspected terrorists and those associated with terrorist organizations. *See* USA PATRIOT Act, Pub. L. No. 107-56, 115 Stat. 272 (2001).

74 117 Cong. Rec. 31535, 31550 (1971).

75 *Hearing on H.R. 234 and other Bills Prohibiting Detention Camps Before the House Committee on the Judiciary,* 92nd Cong., 1971, 79 (hereafter "Hearings").

76 H.R. Rep. No. 92-116, at 2.

77 50 U.S.C. § 813(a) (1970). The legislative findings preceding the Act stated that a "world Communist movement," organized on a conspiratorial basis, and with the support of the most powerful enemy nation of the United States, had sent agents to enter the United States and engage in "treachery . . . espionage, sabotage, [and] terrorism." Internal Security Act of 1950, Pub. L. No. 831, 81st Cong., 2d Sess. (September 23, 1950) at §§ 2(1), 2(7), 101(1), 101(6). "Congress passed the Emergency Detention Act . . . to lay the groundwork for any future need to detain large groups of people in times of emergency.

A number of the [Japanese-American] detention camps were 'mothballed' for future use." Joel B. Grossman, "The Japanese American Cases and the Vagaries of Constitutional Adjudication in Wartime: An Institutional Perspective," *University of Hawaii Law Review*, 19, 649, 664 (1997).

78 H.R. Rep. No. 92–116, at 2.

79 Ibid. at 5.

80 Ibid. at 2.

81 *Howe v. United States*, 452 U.S. 473, 479 n.3 (1981) (emphasis in original).

82 U.S. Const. art. I, § 8. cl. 11.

83 *See Brown v. United States*, 12 U.S. (8 Cranch) 110, 115–16 (1814) (holding that the president could not seize, as enemy property, material found on U.S. land at the commencement of hostilities in 1812 without congressional authority). Indeed, the Supreme Court, early in its history, affirmed a congressional statute that limited the president's power during wartime to seize ships on the high seas that were thought to be aiding the enemy. *See Little v. Barreme*, 6 U.S. (2 Cranch) 170 (1804) (finding that presidential order did not make seizures legal).

84 *Myers v. United States*, 272 U.S. 52 (1926).

85 U.S. Const. art. II, § 3.

86 *See, e.g., Loving v. United States*, 517 U.S. 748, 758 (1996). ("[T]he lawmaking function belongs to Congress . . . and may not be conveyed to another branch or entity.") *See also Field v. Clark*, 143 U.S. 649, 692 (1892). ("That Congress cannot delegate legislative power to the President is a principle universally recognized as vital to the integrity and maintenance of the system of government ordained by the Constitution.")

87 *Youngstown*, 343 U.S. at 588. ("The President's order does not direct that a congressional policy be executed in a manner prescribed by Congress—it directs that a presidential policy be executed in a manner prescribed by the President.")

88 *Youngstown*, 343 U.S. at 655 (Jackson, J., concurring).

89 U.S. Const. art. I, § 7, cl. 2.; *INS v. Chadha*, 462 U.S. 919, 954 (1983).

90 *Chadha*, 462 U.S. at 951.

91 U.S. Const. art. I, § 9, cl. 2 (the "Suspension Clause").

92 *Ex parte Merryman*, 17 F. Cas. 144, 149 (C.C.D. Md. 1861) (No. 9487) (Taney, C.J.).

93 Jose Padilla is being held in the naval brig at Goose Creek, South Carolina, which, according to the *Wall Street Journal*, has a special wing that could be used to house up to twenty citizens as "enemy combatants." *See* Jess Bravin, "More Terror Suspects may Sit in Limbo," *Wall Street Journal*, August 8, 2002, A4. Administration officials have indicated that their ultimate plan may be broader, proposing camps where citizens could be interned and subject to military detention on the decision of a committee of the attorney general, the secretary of defense, and the director of the CIA. *See* Jonathan Turley, "Ashcroft's Hellish Vision," *Los Angeles Times*, August 14, 2002, pt. 2, 11.

94 Enhanced civil judicial process has generally been held adequate to strip naturalized citizenship in certain circumstances. *See Schneiderman v. United States*, 320 U.S. 118, 123, 160 (1943) ("clear and convincing" standard); cf. *Gorbach v. Reno*, 219 F.3d 1087, 1098–99 (9th Cir. 2000) (en banc) (rejecting administrative denaturalization process); *Osborn v. Bank of the United States*, 22 U.S. (9 Wheat.) 738, 827 (1824) (Naturalized citizen "becomes

a member of the society, possessing all the rights of a native citizen, and standing, in the view of the constitution, on the footing of a native. *The Constitution does not authorize Congress to enlarge or abridge those rights.*").

In contrast, loss of birth citizenship is now limited to voluntary renunciation. *See Afroyim v. Rusk,* 387 U.S. 253, 267-68 (1967). (Native-born citizen may not be expatriated by Congress involuntarily, overruling *Perez v. Brownell, 356 U.S. 44, 1958,* and affirming "constitutional right to remain a citizen . . . unless [the citizen] voluntarily relinquishes that citizenship.") *See also Kennedy v. Martinez-Mendoza*, 372 U.S. 144 (1963) (holding, prior to *Afroyim*, that criminal process guarantees apply to punitive statute stripping citizenship of draft evaders).

On the need for civilian judicial review of the issue of citizenship generally, *see Agosto v. INS*, 436 U.S. 748 753 (1978) ("the Constitution requires that there be some provision for de novo judicial determination of claims to American citizenship in deportation proceedings"); *Smith v. Shaw*, 12 Johnson 257 (N.Y. Sup. Ct. Jud. 1815) (a court-martial has no jurisdiction to try the question of prisoner's citizenship; detaining officer liable in tort for detention without subject-matter jurisdiction).

95 *See* U.S. Const. Art. III, § 3.

96 "It is the observation of the celebrated Montesquieu, that if the crime of treason be indeterminate, this alone is sufficient to make any government degenerate into arbitrary power." Robert Green McCloskey, ed, *The Works of James Wilson* (Cambridge, Mass.: Harvard University Press, 1967), Vol. 2, 663.

97 *Perez v. Brownell*, 356 U.S. 44, 64 (1958) (Warren, C.J., dissenting).

12

Poem For My Mother

By a relative of one of the Yemeni detainees at Guantánamo

POEM FOR MY MOTHER

You ask me how my mother lives—
Please do not wait to hear.
You ask me how my mother lives—
Words cannot speak her tears.

I know not even where to start,
Which door might open to
The darkness in my mother's heart
Blacked out by censored cards.

My mother's heart remains a void
Yet papered round with pain
My mother's heart remains a void
Since Yasein went away.

My mother's body struggles on;
World, watch her burning soul.
My mother's body struggles on,
With sorrow as her shrine.

My mother names before our God
The cause of all her pain
My mother kneels in prayer to God
As tears run down her eyes.

You ask me how my mother lives—
Please do not wait to hear.
My mother's heart swells larger than
Mere language can declare.

About the Authors

REED BRODY is special counsel at Human Rights Watch (HRW). He is the author of the HRW report *The Road to Abu Ghraib*, which examines the roots of the Iraqi prisoner abuse scandal. Brody coordinated HRW's intervention in the case of Augusto Pinochet in Britain's House of Lords, and initiated and coordinates the prosecution of the former dictator of Chad, Hissène Habré, who was arrested on torture charges in Senegal. Previously, he led UN teams investigating massacres in the Democratic Republic of Congo and observing human rights conditions in El Salvador. In 1995–1996, he coordinated an international legal team to prosecute human rights crimes in Haiti. He is co-author (with Michael Ratner) of *The Pinochet Papers: The Case of Augusto Pinochet in the British and Spanish Courts*, and author of *Tibet: Human Rights and the Rule of Law* and *Contra Terror in Nicaragua*.

RACHEL MEEROPOL is an attorney at the Center for Constitutional Rights. She completed her undergraduate degree at Wesleyan University in 1997 and graduated from NYU Law School in 2002. Ms. Meeropol is currently vice president of the New York City chapter of the National Lawyers Guild.

BARBARA OLSHANSKY is the deputy director for litigation and organizing of the Center for Constitutional Rights. Ms. Olshansky graduated from Stanford Law School in 1985 and clerked for two years for Rose E. Bird, chief justice of the California Supreme Court. She is coauthor of *Against War with Iraq* and author of *Secret Trials and Executions*.

MICHAEL RATNER is president of the Center for Constitutional Rights. Among his many cases was the successful closing of the camp for HIV-positive Haitian refugees at Guantánamo Bay Naval Station, Cuba, and numerous cases challenging a president's authority to go to war without congressional approval. He coauthored the book *Against War with Iraq* and wrote chapters in *Freedom at Risk, It's a Free Country*, and *Lost Liberties*. He was a lecturer at Yale Law School and currently teaches at Columbia Law School. He has served as president of the National Lawyers Guild and special counsel to Haitian president Jean-Bertrand Aristide to assist in the prosecution of human rights crimes.

STEVEN MACPHERSON WATT is a human rights fellow with the Center for Constitutional Rights. Since November 2001, he has coordinated the Center's litigation efforts in relation to government measures adopted post-9/11. Originally from Scotland, Mr. Watt qualified and practiced law in that country and holds an LL.M in international human rights law from the University of Notre Dame.

Index